OTHER BOOKS BY DON SCHOFIELD

Of Dust (chapbook), 1991
Approximately Paradise, 2002,
Kindled Terraces: American Poets in Greece (anthology), 2004
The Known: Selected Poems [of Nikos Fokas] *1982 – 2000* (translation), 2010
Before Kodachrome, 2012
In Lands Imagination Favors, 2014
The Flow of Wonder (chapbook), 2018

A DIFFERENT HEAVEN

NEW AND SELECTED POEMS

DON SCHOFIELD

DOS MADRES

2023

DOS MADRES PRESS INC.
P.O. Box 294, Loveland, Ohio 45140
www.dosmadres.com   editor@dosmadres.com

Dos Madres is dedicated to the belief that the small press is essential
to the vitality of contemporary literature as a carrier of the new voice,
as well as the older, sometimes forgotten voices of the past. And in an
ever more virtual world, to the creation of fine books pleasing to the
eye and hand.

Dos Madres is named in honor of Vera Murphy and Libbie Hughes,
the "Dos Madres" whose contributions have made this press possible.

Dos Madres Press, Inc. is an Ohio Not For Profit Corporation and a
501 (c) (3) qualified public charity. Contributions are tax deductible.

Executive Editor: Robert J. Murphy

Illustration & Book Design: Elizabeth H. Murphy
www.illusionstudios.net

Typeset in Adobe Garamond Pro & Trajan Pro
ISBN 978-1-953252-86-9
Library of Congress Control Number: 2023940243

ACKNOWLEDGEMENTS

Border Lines: Poems of Migration (Everyman's Library,
          Knopf 2020*)*: "Migrant Stories"
Circumference: "Menses and the Sea" (Translation)
Crazyhorse: "Bird of Death" (Translation)
Crosswinds: *Should We Go to Mars??*
The High Window: "Holiday," "Lost in Place," "Voices, Good
          Friday, Hotel Diafani" and "Blinds."
Mudfish (Finalist, Mudfish Poetry Prize 2020): "No Elsewhere"
Naugatuck River Review: "Eternal Adolescence"
Nowhere Magazine (Finalist, Fall 2019 Travel Writing
          Contest): "After the Firestorms"
Poeticanet: "The Poet at Eight" (under the title "Departures")
Reed Magazine 2021 Chapbook: "Athens Snow"
San Diego Poetry Anthology: "Bongos"
Seneca Review: "The Adolescence of Forgetfulness" (Translation)
          (Nominated for a Pushcart Prize)
Southword (Runner Up, 2021 Gregory O'Donoghue
          International Poetry Prize): "Mass Graves, Hart Island"
Suisun Valley Review: "Mytiline Notebook"

*Poems in this book have been selected from the following
  previous collections of mine:*

BOOK-LENGTH:
     •*Approximately Paradise* (University Press of Florida, 2002);
     •*Before Kodachrome* (FutureCycle Press, 2012); and
     •*In Lands Imagination Favors* (Dos Madres Press, 2014).

CHAPBOOKS:
     •*Of Dust* (March Street Press, 1991) and
     • *The Flow of Wonder* (Kelsay Books, 2018)

TRANSLATION:
     • *The Known: Selected Poems* [of Nikos Fokas]*, 1981 – 2000*
       (Ypsilon/Books, Athens, 2010).

For all those who helped make Greece home,
especially Dennis, who opened the door,
and Aleka, whose love warms the hearth.

TABLE OF CONTENTS

▦ TRANSLATIONS

NEW POEMS

ATHENS SNOW

I'm startled as I wake
        by the stark silence
of morning. No dogs barking,
        no cars starting,
only the whisper of snow
        swirling in a March wind,

From Mt. Penteli
        all the way out to the islands,
the radio says, and here,
        drifts inching up doorways and sills,
weighing down the mimosas,
        the garden's urns
losing their form, the marble grapes
        of a fountain
        iced over. It's easy

to lie here and remember
        in another country, another time,
nuns telling us in school
        how each flake is unique,
as we watched them fall, so delicate,
        into anonymous mounds.

Drifts could pile so high
        they once kept our family cabin
snowed-in for days. We listened to the radio
        till the batteries died,

then clawed out
        to an all-white landscape—
no road, no car, the apple trees
        in the orchard below
crowned and glittering,
        the whole mountainside
still as our breath
        hovering in front of us

—till that buck
        stepped out from behind the shed,
clumps of ice
        hanging from his antlers, ears twitching,
eyes glaring, hungry and cold;
        then he bounded up the slope
through chest-high drifts.

        Now I gaze at the marble Athena
on my neighbor's balcony—
        a bas-relief
of the goddess grieving,
        pressing her forehead
to her spear, snow on her cheek and breasts,
        little ridges on her raised arm,
the tip of her helmet. Soon

        all of her will be covered
        in a formless mound
as my own body
        grows heavy with years. Snow builds

in the quiet wind
        just as each
singular moment
        falls to endless
drifts of time, at their core

        a darkness, a pulsing sentience
        with the eyes of that buck
determined to go into
        the glittering present.

LOST IN PLACE

Náousa Bay, Kythnos

Sitting on this porch overlooking the sea,
I want to exist, to know for sure
I exist. When I walk the beach,

waves caress my feet, recede
with a long, slow hiss. I can't say
what gulls know, or crabs. I only know,
right now, this porch, where my chest
rises and falls with each new breath,
each desire. Does that mean I exist?

*

Beyond the beach there's a garden with pears
and lemons, snakes and scorpions, all night
a chorus of bullfrogs deep within the cistern,
sad hooting from poplars and pines. Do they know
they exist? Each morning

my neighbor tosses lambs
onto the back of his battered pickup
as they cry, *I aam, I aam.*

*

When I climb the rocky path to the village, goats stare
but don't really care. Skinny mules with heavy loads
pass by, dropping their rose-shaped turds
without stopping. Cicadas grind away
the afternoon. I want their sudden wings
after so many years underground, their brilliant trilling,
again and again: *I exist.*

*

Coming down from Driopída,
I see my neighbors' whitewashed houses,
blue shutters, red-tiled roofs, and see them again
wholly reflected on the sea's smooth surface,
but fresher, newer. Now I'm the boy again,
tossing and turning in a dream
of soft-legged waves. Borne
by those legs, I glide
to the edge of a drystone wall
with stones tall as doors. I knock
and go in.

*

In the shallows where I swim,
I lie on the ripples of sand, let my body
sway with the current, feel its warmth
wash over me, through me. No matter how deeply
I settle into the sand, how many fish
swirl around me, crabs nudge
my legs, my cheek, I know
no *I* can hold me for long.

*

Here on my porch,
where existence is determined by nothing
but rhythm, where at dusk I'm lulled
by the fading trill of cicadas, the pulsing necks
of lizards stretching toward the setting sun,
awake, but barely, all the *Is* of ants
still coming and going,

surely we all exist.

The lambs cry out, *I aam, I aam.*
Mule turds drop—
nope,
nope.

MYTILINE NOTEBOOK

Summer days of stillness,
watching flies in their slowness,

days that remind me
of the Greek for still life,
nekrí físi, dead nature.

*

Each morning the flies come
to where I sit on my balcony
writing in the light of the world,
the wonder of quiet
except for their buzzing.

Eventually, one lands
at the edge of my notebook,
flittering and jittering, forelegs like diligent fingers
gathering nothing, mouth nibbling nothing.

I cup my hand, hold still
as a still life,

and try to catch it.

*

Walking at dusk, I recall the local word
for twilight, *lykófos, wolf-light.* That's the hour

wolves dart out. I can hear
their long howls, smell their sour breath
as they circle my thoughts, clawing at my fears and beliefs,
dreams and desires, until there's nothing left for the mind
to protect. And all the while wolf-light
pours over me, dragging me
deeper into the dark, till I'm lost
among the lost, the stillborn and damned. Then a star appears,
as if night's canopy has sprung a leak.
Another. Then another.

*

Some mornings I wake in the early dark,
go out to my balcony and wait for sunrise.

The light that comes over the horizon
is thin, almost brittle, as it touches
the mountain behind me,
the gardens and orchards below,
red-tiled roofs along the sea,
then the whole expanse
of sleeping bay.

*

When the sun's at its zenith,
I leave my writing and go down to the sea,
sit at the beach's one taverna
behind a curtain of octopi
and buzzing flies,
drink an ouzo, maybe two. I do this

every day, then walk back up
the mountain. Always there's a donkey
tied to the shade of an olive tree,
or a ram rising up on his hind-legs
to get to the unripe pears. He has,
when he turns to look at me,
the golden eyes of a goat-god.

The rows of cypresses I pass
are dark green flames, torches
planted in the earth
all the way up to my room.
They hint at an afterlife
I've never believed in, though now,
dizzy from ouzo
and the aroma of fennel and thyme,
I might just change my mind,

*

might stay right here, in dead nature,
writing outside of time,

putting down my pen
now and then, to sit still
as a still life....

But here, you can't catch the flies.
I've tried.
   In dead nature,
they're the quickest of all.

BLINDS

You can spot us in this tall, rough-wood blind,
binoculars in hand, scanning
the Xirolímni Lagoon, disputing in whispers
the genera of grebes and cormorants, ignoring
the graceless mud hens. You can tell we're humans
by our short-billed caps,
how excited we get when at last
the last cranes step out.

One's neck is a sideways S
reflected on the murky ripples. Another preens
with sure, quick motions in a casual,
Sunday-morning way. A third, eyes close to the water,
searches for movement—a tail's flick,
a surface break. When a fourth lifts its wings,
they're up and off, gliding across the marsh
toward the open sea. Only the mud hens remain.

Like us, they're part of late autumn solitude.

*

Every year, before the ice sets in,
thousands of kokanee salmon
fight their way up the Flathead River
to McDonald Creek. Every year

bald eagles, twenty, thirty to a tree,
settle on the oaks along both banks.

And every year dozens of us drive
hundreds of miles to ascend these blinds,
click photos of weary salmon laying eggs
on the creekbed's gravel. The eagles swoop in,

screeching as they scoop up their half-
dead prey, then perch on the tallest branches,
leisurely tearing the flesh of these that can't help

but return to this place of birth
and death. Birth and death,
with nothing in between

but feasting raptors and we with our cameras
witnessing the vexed pulsing of instinct,
the gluttonous pleasure of magnificent predators.

Cameras full,
we make our way home.

*

One night in Nepal's southern jungle, our hotel guide led
us, single-file, along a hard-dirt path, in stocking-feet, while
another group filed past us, on their way back to the vans.
In strict silence we entered a narrow concrete blind under
layers of creepers and vines, took our places, three to each
window, and gazed out at a floodlit clearing: a tiger eating
what remained of a baby water buffalo tied to a stake.

Too late, we only caught the end as she tossed a thigh-bone
high in the air, rolled in blood and purred as she licked the
remaining flesh from her fur.

Five minutes, then we filed out for the next group to file in.

*

As the story goes, Buddha,
in an earlier incarnation,
was walking the jungle one morning
when he came upon a starving tiger
ready to eat her dying cubs.

The Buddha, willing to sacrifice himself
so the tiger wouldn't devour her own young,
laid down in front of her.

She couldn't even lift one paw,
so he grabbed a bamboo shaft,
cut his own throat—

not to save humankind,
just to lie there, a man weary of suffering,
even that of a tiger and her cubs,

and before he did, he let out a howl—

a mournful sound to you and me
in our reader's blind,

but to her, a gentle lure.

Eternal Adolescence

Goat Dance, Skyros Mardi Gras

Who can sing, *I'm still, I'm still, I'm still the boy,*
sleeping beneath rocks, refusing to molt, as if caught
in some old longing? We're ready to rise like we did
last year, like we do every year,

wearing cloaks of goatskins and goat-bells
tied around our waists, fifty kilos or more,
drinking and singing, raising our crooks up high,
the masks on our faces—skins of slaughtered lambs.

The music is ancient with sobbing, our breath drenched
with stench, our bodies dragged down by the weight of bells,
swaying and pitching like elephants, one against
the other. The last one standing is a hero for the year.

We cling to this childhood dream though the smell of the masks
is unbearable and none of this brings beginnings,
not the clinking of bottles, the clanking of bells, the bagpipes.
whining past dawn. Bodies numb, we let the earth

pull us back. We can't rise with that song we once sang.

VOICES, GOOD FRIDAY, HOTEL DIAFANI

Their website promised, "Pastoral,"
"Authentic," "A Spiritual Experience,"
but what did I get?—

broken window frames
piled on the balcony, lightbulbs dangling
from the ceiling, a rooster's bland crowing
all afternoon, a bleating lamb
tied to the garage next door.

Yianni's lamb. Tomorrow, he says,
he'll straddle that lamb, twist tight its neck,
slice through to the back of its throat,
warm blood flowing as Foula, his wife,
extracts intestines for a soup they'll have
after Midnight Mass, once the priest
has lit all the villagers' candles, and each family
has walked the flame home, made a cross
of smoke above their door.

Then they'll break the fast
with a soup that tastes like it sounds

(say it),

Magirítsa.

*

Let me visit the other guests:

These with no decisions but manners—
what place, which platter, grapes or pine seeds?

These with gilded faces
dark as that cistern on Chios, no light,
not a ray among the columns, just the knowledge
a thousand women drowned there.

These the ten thousand
hoplites passing in supplication,
the gates closed at Barate Larande, Sardês.
The Satrap at Calper was our pal, would've let us stay
forever, all the wine and millet, cattle and barley,
ponies in our gardens, triremes on a lake, the grace of their women
as they served us, as they spread their golden coverlets.

All perfect?

Not quite. No olives.

*

4 am. The village square
quiet. From my balcony I hear
one voice rising from smoldering embers:

I am weary
of the flames, pants and shirt
stuffed with straw, sack with painted eyes
for a face, body dangling

over a pyre of burning logs, the whole village
throwing firecrackers, a whole
year's anger—
                    I am why
you mingled with the crowd all night,
searching face to face—
not for a part in the ritual,
the easy flow of outrage—

but for a kiss
on your cheek, one word
whispered in your ear,

"Master."

Holiday

Walking a cobbled lane in Trastevere,
we stopped for a drink at a café-bar
with wobbly tables. As usual those days,

we were fighting, which means
we weren't talking. I was thinking

of that Roman prison we'd visited that morning,
of the men our guide had said
were crucified upside down there—
St. Peter and bar Giora—

while she was watching a beggar
flit, one table to the next. Reaching

for her purse, she spilled her gin-tonic
on her blouse, her skirt, her brand new Il Gancio
leather jacket. She straddled her chair

as I knelt beside her trying to wipe off her skirt,
that jacket, while that beggar
leaned in, palm outstretched—

Can't you see we have a problem! I snapped.

No, he replied, in perfect English,
That's not a problem.

Mass Graves, Hart Island

> "Hart Island is the domain of the
> dispossessed, where the poorest and most
> marginalized citizens are laid to rest...."
> —*New York Times,* April 29, 2020

The unclaimed dead in their plywood coffins
sway a little as hooks and chains
lower them into long
muddy trenches; forklifts
stack them neatly. Soon billowing smoke
darker than night
descends over the island
as great earth-movers
cover the mass graves,
their only mourners
oily wavelets
lapping the shore
and one voiceless angel
who keeps circling this small,
treeless island
sinking under the weight
of a million unwanted souls,
her mercy, now and forever,
unspoken.

SHOULD WE GO TO MARS??

Protest sign, Idomeni refugee camp,
northern Greece

Whole families pushing wobbly shopping carts
against wind and rain, balancing our bundled belongings
on heads already heavy with history, we've come
to this muddy field of stubble at the border,
the border closed.

*

We hang our wet clothes
along the chain-link fences you built,
stand in line to shower, to eat,
in line again to charge our phones and calm
each other down, no news from home.

*

You who built these fences will flee
bombs too one day, book passage on
a leaking dinghy, wedge your pliant body
between two-hundred others. Soon, water gone,
motor dead, boat sinking, life-jackets worthless,
you'll see how men, women and children hold on.
Or not.

*

We plod this camp's
one dirt road, part like the Dead Sea
when your trucks filled with charity
arrive, your convoys of politicians and photographers
eager for pictures of our wives
in black hijabs, our daughters pushing empty
strollers, our husbands sitting in mud, telling stories
and arguing over where to cross the frenzied border river,
how many times our neighborhoods have been bombed to rubble,
if we'll always be this powerless.

*

Our children follow beside your cars, pressing thin foreheads
against your rolled-up windows, not begging, just foraging.
They raise one finger as they look inside. *One,*
they call out, *One,* meaning one of whatever
you might have, one Chiclet or one
of the beeping phones on your dash, one of the cameras
in your laps, or maybe that empty seat beside you, one ticket
to another life.

*

One day your children's children will marry ours. By then,
the planet stropped by storms, whole cities and forests
toppled and burning, dead bodies disgorged
into the boiling sea, we'll all be telling the same story:

how, together, with crates of lemons, bundles
of yellowed books describing how
to navigate the stars, weighed down even more
by history, we'll all board a jerry-
rigged spaceship, wobble off to Mars.

ONE OF THE DEAD, 1969

For Donnie Parker

Sure, I popped the clutch, hit the gas and now we're racing
up Clay, down Jackson, four in the morning, no cops,
no cars, just blinking red lights I ignore. And yeah,

I hear you yelling, *Donnie stop, you'll kill us both!*
our bodies bouncing and jolting as we fishtail
toward North Beach. It's not me at the wheel,

but the door-gunner of a *HueyCobra*
taking out the Viet Cong in the jungle below,
the guy who paints his face to walk point on patrol,

who keeps count of the bunks on base emptying
one by one, some grunts transferred, some hit by mines,
some fragging a lieutenant and slipping away.

I'm home now, I know, since everyone keeps saying,
Get a job. Find a girl. You'll be okay. But hey,
bullets keep popping in my head. I wake

praying it's not me who got hit but the guy in front
or behind. When I roll out of bed, the horde of myself
rolls with me. If I go for a walk, *Dragonflies* drop bombs

lawn to lawn, and in the park there's a sniper's nest
in every tree. Some nights I sit on my porch
wanting to believe I've found some peace. But what's here

ain't peace, only rules I'm supposed to obey, all the while,
beneath the calm, a fuse slowly burns. When I stay to watch
the stars disappear, those I killed are there beside me.

I feel their breath on my cheek, their strong hands
lifting my shoulders, like they did when I was lying in mud,
facedown, bleeding out. I hear someone whisper

yet again, *Let your body be true to something more*
than the man. Give it to the shifting winds....
So I'll leave you now, leave my car

racing downhill. You'll grab the wheel, I know,
hit the brakes. You're the real hero here, my friend. And of course
you'll come back to hold my bleeding head in your lap

as one of the horde says a few more words: *Got it right*
at last! From my sniper's nest here
on the curb, I can taste the wind, smell the trace

of burning flesh in the air. So, yeah,
the body can be so much more....

No Elsewhere

For Dennis Schmitz, 1937-2019

I keep seeing him in dreams
walking the edge of an Iowa cornfield
or sitting on a rain-slicked curb

in Chicago, the look on his face as if waiting
for the irony to hit. Sometimes I see
a slow creek heading west,

hear the sound of vowels cascading
down the page in a cold garage, his cast-
iron typewriter clacking, ribbon rising

like that stream in winter lapping the shore
when each letter hits, the words he worked to the bone
no better than the *dahs* at the tip of his tongue.

*

When the amniotic fluid breaks,
he knew, the body becomes a cage,
a trap. What lasts is that fossil we call

the soul, and the grind of aging joints
impersonal as rocks scattered in a field.
He's cut but not cut down, happy to be

part elm, part oak and pine, happier still
to be sleeping in the body of the boy he was
those long, slow, summer mornings.

*

How to fill that void when what I feel
for him, mentor and friend, smolders
in every cell of my body?

*

Sometimes what's intimate, he wrote,
only means there's no elsewhere.
But what's here, right now, is what is missing—

round head, short hair, sharp eyes. *No elsewhere.*
Riding his bike, shooting his hook. *No elsewhere.*
Quiet laugh, quick puns. *No elsewhere.*

*

He left drafts of poems scattered throughout
his house that last night he tucked his bones
to bed, still balancing on a ladder of humans,

I imagine, waiting for the irony to hit.
Or maybe he was gazing at motes of dust
drifting between shifting truths, playing

with prisms of light in tall beveled windows.

THE POET AT EIGHT

As you wake, the boy's just gone to sleep.
If he sits up and calls you, you should come, you're his father.

But it's okay, take your cap and logbook, your holster
and hole-punch. Take all the grey that's a Greyhound uniform.

By now he's heard all your stories, understands
why you prefer the depot, its dispatchers calling out

arrivals, departures. He sees you there,
smiling vaguely, punching tickets as your passengers board.

You're Nevada bound, though he likes to see you as Charon
taking shades to the underworld. Climbing Donner Pass,

all the souls asleep, you're Captain of this vessel.
No sleep for you, though sometimes, as the motor drones,

wipers flap, toggles glow across the dash,
your leg gets so numb you can barely feel the clutch,

and sometimes, crossing the Truckee River, your eyelids
getting heavier and heavier, you wonder if he's awake yet,

if he ever thinks of you. Can't you see,
you've made him just like yourself, always dreaming of departures.

So go ahead, drift toward any snow-lined precipice.
He'll be okay. Whether you make it to Reno or not,

he'll be standing on his bed, on one leg, his crumpled sheets
a lagoon of flamingos he's imagined, preening in first light.

By the time you arrive at the depot, they'll be taking off,
dazzling the darkness of his room with their black underwings,

the soft pink of their breasts. As you collect
the silver dollars from each passenger's eyes,

they'll be flying the River Styx, calling and calling.

I Didn't Go to My Father's Funeral

In the depths of my sleep, the sound of crashing waves.
If there's a ship in my dream, it must find its way
to southern Spain, or else I'll wake in a haze,

thinking of the men carrying my father
on their shoulders. It's not sadness I'll feel as they lower him
into the earth, just a dim kind of happiness

since I know, however hurtful and absent he was,
he's going to a place where the light is pure and clear,
even as I know, of course, there's no such place.

Now a priest fills the air with prayer, just words,
the clash of vowels up against consonants,
like that sea in my dreams, that ship chugging south.

Some nights there's a moon above that sea, hovering
like my father's unshaven face in the mirror.
I want to touch that face again, feel his lips

coming in close to kiss me. Like he did so long ago.
After that just words, vowels against consonants,
his voice droning on, his face that moon

getting smaller and smaller. Then crashing waves.
That ship trying to make its way to southern Spain.

WASHER MUSIC

For my stepmother

She rises each morning, vacuum blaring, washer moaning,
fills her hours with dusting the Disney knickknacks
on the mantle, smoothing doilies on tables and armchairs,
couch and window sills, polishing dressers, linoleum and tiles,
till everything shines like lost Nebraska. After dinner,
dishes done, she sits in her corner of the sofa,
crocheting, watching the neighbors come and go,
reciting all their failures without mercy. Ours too.

I'm that damn California brat who dirties her towels,
leaves handprints on mirrors and walls, tangles the phone cord
beyond recognition. Sprawled in front of the TV
each evening, I hate those clacking needles,
the intricate hearts and snowflakes she knits, hate even more
my father's nonstop praise for her. Taking my bath,
I slosh suds, make lopping waves that splash and spill.
Tiny boat of my life, I pray, *please take me away.*

For Dad, she's a comfort in middle-age—never again
those gloomy Motel 6s, whiskey and solitaire till dawn.
As long as he keeps the screen door closed, wipes his feet,
never brings any dark friends home, there's meat on the table,
a garden with canaries and a flowery chaise-lounge. He snores
on that lounge or on the couch when home, the man of the house
barely opening his eyes as he shuffles off to bed.

That's when she starts the day's last load of laundry,
then sits at her mirror, letting down her hair and thinking
of home. She's forgotten how dust would swirl in relentless waves
across the barren fields, men and boys tromp
through the house with muddy boots. It's the cleanliness she recalls,
how her daily toiling was a kind of rectitude.
Before she lies down, she brushes her long silver hair
to washer music, certain Nebraska and Heaven are one.

BONGOS

"...I hung on like death:
Such waltzing was not easy."
—Theodore Roethke

At twelve I'd go through the house pounding tables and chairs,
doorways and lampshades, maybe from anger, maybe
from eagerness to be with this family I'd lived with before,
though divorce was now in the air. I pounded so much
that mother bought me bongos. At first I'd hit them
with my fists, knowing all was about to collapse,
then began working hard at keeping a rhythm going
since one day soon, I knew, she'd put me on a bus
back to my father, my real father, no father at all.

That was Fresno, where I learned to drum with calloused palms,
aching wrists, faster and faster, harder and harder,
to beat back loss before it could come. I was sure
nothing in the world could save me but bongos, that all I wanted
was to be with that Cherokee house-painter in his fifties,
that soft-spoken Italian in her twenties, to be the child
they could never have, even if he'd come home drunk,
beat me with the palm of his hand till she'd
intervene; then he'd lift me to his shoulders, totter room to room,
singing out love for me, for her, for the entire world,
then send me off, with one last swat, to bed.

All night I'd tap at my chest to find a rhythm
that could calm my aching, frightened heart. I could feel
her love shifting away, something else inside me
rising to take its place, pushing me to pound
even more, some yearning to beat down a door, step into

another life, where love isn't fear, where there's more
for a boy of twelve than this craving for a mother not his,
a father who can beat him and love him at the same time.

On that afternoon express to Sacramento,
convinced it was my fault they split up, I kept tapping a dull rhythm
on the armrest, *no home, no home.* Then I knew what to do:
there, on that crowded Greyhound, I started pounding
my bare knees, faster and faster, louder and louder,
skin against skin, elbows, wrists, fists and palms,
riveting my heart to a place where love never fails,
where in contrapuntal rhythm, hands blur, knees sway.

AFTER THE FIRESTORMS

Driving the two hours from SFO to Sonoma,
dull haze of smoke getting thicker and thicker
the farther north I go, past singed rows of grapevines,
charred oaks, scorched swathes of wild rye,
white gaps in the burnt landscape where houses once stood,
the muted reds and golds of late fall not beautiful,

I think of my brother
hobbling through the kitchen with his walker,
arguing with his wife, no doubt, over who will sleep
with who, not him with her, not ever these days,
but me with him.

All those summers I travelled to Reno
to visit Mom, it was him I'd go for, my good-looking,
fast-living big brother, slicked-back hair and bell-bottoms,
swaggering down Virginia Street any hour,
day or night, playing the penny-slots near the sidewalk,
flirting with the showgirls in the gilded alleys,
skin ablaze in Reno neon.

Again I'll be sleeping with him, my smallness, as always,
beside his largeness. These days he slumps in his armchair
and stares at the TV, silent in the face of lost hope,
failed love, or so I imagine as I pull up to their house,
see their porch light at dusk, too dim
to be Reno neon. The hunched clouds of smoke
are not from last year's firestorms, but bigger fires
up north, where all of Paradise is burning.

Late November. A Thai restaurant.
I'm here with my brother's wife and his youngest son.
We've ordered noodles with cashews, eggplant with pork
and spring rolls. They're talking low, almost in harmony:

We love your brother, but he wears us out.
Won't walk. Won't take his pills. Won't eat what he should.
And it's so blessed quiet when he does go out.
No coughing. No wheezing. No clanging walker.

He moved to Texas, his son explains while the waitress
lays out steaming bowls, *fell from his pickup*
and broke two vertebrae. I had to go get him.
Sullen and angry the whole way back,
when he saw his own bed, he laid down and cried.

He was living with our sister, I remind them
as the waitress pours us more tea, *All his life*
she's been trying to control him.
Can't you let him do what he wants?

You don't understand! my nephew insists,
We're faced with coming home and finding him dead.
Like last year, his mother adds, *He doctor-shopped*
for pain pills. We found him on the kitchen floor.

That's his way of rebelling, I counter, *His best years are over*
and he knows it. Let him make his own mistakes. It's his
goddamned life anyway....

33

In the searing light of this shopping-center restaurant,
we argue over what's best for my brother, her husband,
his dad, till the waitress brings our check, asks
if we want a doggie-bag for the spring rolls.

~

He came here to recover from a hip operation,
clutching his wife's arm and moaning,

I'm gonna die here, I know it.
Maybe he was right.

This center for physical therapy
is also a nursing home. Death visits often.

*

When I visit, there's a guy who likes to stop in front of me,
look intently into my eyes, then shuffle off, laughing loudly.

And a woman who wheels up real close to whisper,
as if sharing a secret, *My son done left me here,*

so long ago I can't remember his name.
What's yours, young man?

*

Today his six weeks are over.
He's at the reception desk, saying good-bye

to a nurse, the pretty one, who just leaned
and kissed him on the cheek,

the one who slaps old codgers,
ever so lightly, when they try to touch her breast.

*

He's not telling me, like he usually does,
how his roommate, first thing each morning,

leans over his bed and touches his cheek—
"To see if you're still alive," the bastard says!

He's not saying a word as we drive away.
He's got that kiss.

~

I've been thinking about his laughter a lot these days
as I watch him maneuver his walker, grunting and moaning,
banging doorways and sills, till he reaches his chair in the living room.
Raspy now, but it can still burst out, quick,
spontaneous, like a flare lighting up the dark. There are days
when all I want is that laugh, especially the mornings
he asks me to help put on his shoes and socks.
He can't bend that far anymore.

So I kneel in front of his bare feet as if they were
some holy relic—white, fine as soft snow,
warm to the touch—slide his socks, first right,
then left, over slightly curling toes, soles

with thin, crisp wrinkles, gently curving heels
and ankles. Then, with a light flick of my fingers,
I tickle both soles, till he laughs and curses me.

How can these be the feet of the boy who walked
barefoot on gravel, kicked pine cones and rocks and once
another boy's face? He makes me stop sometimes,
hunching in pain from his hip and back. There's rage
in his eyes some mornings, harsh glances at whoever else
might be in the room. Still I push and twist
his sneakers over clean white socks, tighten down
the Velcro tongues, and when I'm done, tickle his calf.

Gladness fills my heart as we laugh out loud again,
a tear sliding down my cheek. I could stay right here,
kneeling forever, a good servant caring for his master,
or a mother pampering her child, in this act of submission,
this gesture of love, this prayer.

~

Seeing me through the picture window coming up the walk,
they all rise to greet me—my brother, his wife and two sons,
his son's wife and two children. Hugs and nice words all
around, then we settle into sofas and armchairs. Soon enough,
someone will lean and whisper, to me or whomever, about the
way she dresses, how he brags too much, how she's raising the
grandkids all wrong, and he, though he's studying divinity, is
faking his religion. Dinah's showing me pictures of the roosters
she raises, grand champions though she's only ten. Levi, her
brother, is playing beside her on the sofa with a row of boats.
Larry's watching a game. Ev, Matt and Kacey are in the kitchen.

Come and get it, all three call out, and we, as we enter, see platters piled high with turkey, white meat and dark, steaming bowls of mashed potatoes, shiny gravy-boats, plates of cranberry sauce, two different kinds, baskets of biscuits and cornbread—a crescendo of aromas as we lean to fill our plates. Larry slides his walker, counter to counter, pointing out to Ev what he wants, while I dollop potatoes onto mine, make a hole in the middle—a volcano of pleasure as the gravy overflows—then return to the living room, to the table set up in front of the TV.

For now we don't scrutinize, bicker or complain. We work at keeping the conversation light. I ask Kacey about her job, how the kids are doing in school and she asks about my trip, how many flights, how many hours in the air. Matt and Ev are trading sauces, Levi is dropping bombs onto my plate from a big plastic boat, laughing each time I sound out an explosion. Larry's happy his team is winning. Nate's giggling with his daughter, showing her something on his phone. No need to say anything more than what we do: *Perfect, Splendid, Wonderful.* And if you, Passerby, snuck a look through our big picture window, you'd think you were peering through the Pearly Gates at some heavenly banquet.

If we only knew.

⁓

My brother sits all day watching game-show reruns.
He likes the flashing lights, the jubilant contestants,
the hope he feels before each door opens,
each wheel stops, each countdown hits zero.

Last night his wife asked him again if he wanted
to sleep with her, so I wouldn't have to sleep with him. *No*,
he answered, so quickly it frightened us. So much anger
between them, so little trust, all they can do
is fight distance with distance, a TV in each room.

Bob Barker, can't you make them dream again
of waves lapping the long, warm shore
of the other's body. Gene Rayburn, can't you say, *Get up*
and go to her. Don't say a word. Just hold her
till you feel her body moving with yours. Bob Eubanks,
please whisper, *All night, his lips, your breast.*

Each night she chooses three cats and a queen-size bed,
and he, an overstuffed chair where he can fall asleep
to loud cheers, new winners, all the right answers
even when the questions are wrong.

　⁓

Here in Limbo there's no
explaining the chasms of love,

how my brother in his armchair,
voice cut by phlegm,

can call out each night to his wife
going off to her own bed, *Love you, Ev,*

to his son a little later, *Love you, Matt,*
each one walking away in silence.

Larry says once he gets his mobility back,
he plans to move out. Ev tells me in ten years

she'll retire to a trailer park, a double-wide
with bright new appliances, a door for her cats.

When his parents are gone, Matt intends
to turn this house into a perfect

Airbnb, live in the garage.
Of course they'll all

stay right here,
going to bed each night in silence,

but for Heaven's distant drone.

~

Middle of the night, in the glow of the hall's dim light,
I see feathers strewn across the carpet, Smokey
in the corner licking his paws. Kneeling to gather

the small, grey-white tufts, I imagine some poor,
broken-winged pigeon fallen to the driveway,
shivering in fear. Behind the bathroom door,

something else: a hard, round object, sticky, vaguely warm,
some organ the cat couldn't swallow. Rolling it in my fingers,
I'm sure there's no augury in this egg-shaped ball

wrenched from that pigeon's innards, though indeed
it might be something more, a thing torn
from an avian's inner world. Consider,

as I hold it in my palm, Smokey's quick claws
tearing at that bird's soft underside. Consider the anguish
in its eyes, wings beating furiously as it scuttles

sideways across the lawn, in complete futility.
Consider too Smokey's pride as he licks
the last bits of blood from his paws. And then

consider what's left—this organ, its blunt physicality
beyond the prey's terror, the predator's prowess,
a talisman of sorts, what refuses to be forgotten.

When I drop it into the toilet, it glistens and bobs
as I flush. And flush again.
It's still there.

~

We're sitting at the kitchen table, my brother and I,
talking about Mom, a light rain drumming
the windowpanes. *How quickly the dryness comes,*
she used to say, no matter the season.

And it's true.
When a dry spell hits, grasses whither, stumps
appear in empty fields, everything collapses
into itself. Then the fires come.

Like her, my brother wants his ashes dispersed,
not across the forest floor near the mountain town
where she was born, but into the Truckee River,
from the bridge where as a boy he'd go fishing.

She always lived in mobile homes, a double-wide,
remote inside herself. Each night, after work,
she'd sit in her slip at the kitchen table,
counting the day's tips.

She'd stack them neatly, pour the stacks
into thin paper rolls, tamp them down, seal them tight,
then put them into her purse
to deposit the next day.

Sometimes she'd say, no matter the season, *By God,
we really need some rain. Let it come*, I'd say
if she were here right now, since rain, not fire,
is what the heart really needs right now,

heavy, cleansing rain, slapping windowpanes,
tearing at branches and leaves, pushing through roofs,
into basements, flooding up through floorboards—
downpours
so endless they'll wash us all away.

If she were here right now, she'd sit at this table
all by herself, tally up her losses, make a list
of all she has to do,
get up and do it.

~

He shuffled down the driveway just past dawn,
leaned his walker against my rented car,

gave me a long, deep hug, a quick kiss, told me
he loves me, made me promise to visit more often.

Now I see him in my rearview mirror,
hobbling back up the drive, his face almost golden

in the slanting light. I may never see him again,
I think, as I pass the market, the gas station, turn left

and I'm gone. Can I keep the heartfelt alive, memories
from slipping into shadowy oblivion?

Surely I'll remember last night, helping him from the bathtub,
his soft, pale skin scarred from operations, accidents,

fights in his youth, cuts and lumps from his years
in restaurants and construction, one or two self-inflicted.

His body in that harsh bathroom light is white
as marble, Pentelic marble, used by the ancients

for statues, temples and sarcophagi.

~

Keep driving, I tell myself,
past the scorched barns, the dead live-oaks, the bigleaf
    maples still bare,
past the houses burnt to the ground, the stacks of debris
    still waiting to be carted off.

It's clear that Hell has come to stay.

So limping dogs pick through ash, clutches of chickens
    peck at pale stones.
So this need to go deep into this blackened landscape,
to see every branch that blazed up, every house that
    collapsed in one final gasp,
to feel again my brother's despair, his wife's and son's.

I want to carry them all in my heart,
since I know there's no way back to a life once lived.

So I keep going,
past foals in a charred corral licking raw stubble,
past rows of new fenceposts and freshly poured foundations,
past leaves budding on scorched grapevines stretching all
    the way to the vanishing point,

two hours north, the charred gates of Paradise.

So I keep driving.

From

OF DUST

MORNING (CAIRO)

From the embassies the spotlights shine, sky to ground,
find the owl, the vines, the banyans
along the Nile. A jackal howls

but the man asleep in Room 15
isn't being mourned and no consoling rivers
or carved pillars, only the moon, a dull eye

in deep water. It's enough
to recall the face encased in glass
down the long museum hall

for the man, in his dream, to feel for signs
that might explain his life. What he touches brings on
a longing for sweat landing on stone steps,

a god, embalmed, bundled
in transparent cloth, a procession
toward dead Egypt. He sleeps as dust

rises in the wake of trucks, silence
in bread rising and iron glazing and cars honking,
silence in the windows of buses

dense with eyes
caught in years,
in freighters climbing toward lower Egypt.

Bang of crates. He wakes
with heavy eyelids, as if light
were stone. All the fish leap back

into the dark. All the arms fall away
like heavy reeds, hovering hands
disappear, leaving just his face, null

as the muddy Nile
as he descends the hotel steps
and the stones draw closed.

RESIDENT OF THE OLD CITY

I am not strong. I am faith holding on.
The stone gates I pass through
are thick centuries, the walls scaffolded
to an ancient sleep. This early

only monks pass by,
tall, gaunt Ethiopians
with black robes that flare
like wings as they turn a corner

and are gone. Long before the tourists,
pilgrims gather at the gates
like the dead would
if the dead could leave their long rows
on the hills above the city. They kneel

at the shrines like the old olive trees
of Gethsemane lean their gnarled trunks
toward the sun, offering
meager fruit like votives.

Late afternoon I sit in doorways
with Arab hawkers
who deal in copper, spice, meat
and nuts, who don't know

their daughters have the dark eyes
of mosaics, don't see the Byzantine crosses
in the pocked walls where they play—
and remember as a child
how I kissed the Wailing Wall,

sang a prayer with bobbing head,
followed a line of dancers as they left
the square. The Wall led our joy.
And still the walls lead, past Veronica's veil,
the painted alley where the Armenians live.

And music comes, tourist rock
or *muezzin* at prayer. Wind rattles
and the day fades, only the weightless
rush of dark remains, and a light
in one shop still open. *Come,*

the owner says, *Have tea. My wares
are yours,* as he draws a curtain back
to another at work in the dark. It's the dream
I see, the one that sustains me—

the hammer, the gold, time pounded
into eternity, Herod's throne and Mohammed's dome
amid the rugs, the plates, the flimsy shirts
and hukka smoke, the walls alive
with crosses, crescents and stars.

SURVIVOR OF BABEL

Earns it a man
to climb from earth. Earns it
to face light. Earth
bring moment. Earth
bring dust.

No wing so strong.

*

He rise from me
warm with words but no
the wing. I whisper,

Love, close curtain,
light candle, touch finger
here. Pleasure. Pleasure. Fur
and seeing. He leave

to lug bricks, grapple pulley,
sing choir ascending daily,
storm perfect form God.

*

Wells dry. Houses fallen.
Rubble. No words. Nothing

make sense. I with herd
sit in shade, listen locusts

grind late noon.
Now were you here

we bring in sheep. Now
fill urns. Fingers speak.

Click of tongue.
Nothing make sense. Still

something like words
stones' harsh light,

dust where ewes pass.
Earth no speak.

No wing so strong.

HAGAR IN THE WILDERNESS

"Let me not see the death of the child."
—Genesis

We kissed the icons and left. I carried the child,
bread, a bottle of water. Later
we drank from wells bitter with shards,
ate locusts and scorpions, glad to be gone.
What nations do I want? Only Abraham's
arms on nights the dogs come
to sniff the child. I think of my doll

with corn eyes, the one I rocked
when she was scared—
I built a fire, said a prayer
and pushed her in. She was heavy.
There was nothing more for her
I could do. Under this shrub
he'll stop his crying. The sand
will cover him and he'll be calm.

How the rocks grieve
is not clear, or why
the birds keep circling,
except to remind me the angel
promised Paran with me the queen. I lie
in the sabra and laugh: *Come,*
my wild son, my archer,
this is Paran, we're a nation
of dust.

PIETY

On a post-Byzantine *Madonna and Child*

The Child sits quietly
in the warmth of his mother's
gilded veil. Her breast
is what he wants, white
as a dove. A span of cheek
is all he gets, not enough
to rise from the gilt.

Could a man
step out and not be
one fallen? If gilt
wears away
is it tooled sleep
we see, the thick throats
of the Damned we hear, certain
this age will save them?

If a fig
falls a man
eats it. If a man falls
the ants take him in tiny
mandibles of love,
so the Child would say,
hand raised
in the manner of a blessing.

*

She could hum the totals of grief
for the crumbling who believe
they are rising. Her right eye
is wide, her mouth
tiny, her left eye
so obscure in shadow
it could be ours. We can look in
or out. She has nothing to hide.

There was that moment,
just a memory: light
and a rush of wind
through her mind. She was Eve
and the snake was muttering
when the dove came. It was rain on the sill,
she remembers now. She wanted a dove
so the feathers could remain.

When the believers come
with their motions of piety,
these men tapped into place
by the woman beside them,
they bend and kiss
and amble through their day

never hearing the Satyr
shaking off the night,
sniffing stumps, apples
in clumps. When he lies down again
in the dust, his hooves the hooves
of a lover, she takes him
to her gilded breast
lightly humming.

JOSEPH: A TRIPTYCH

Mary's whispers frighten me. *A child,* she says,
from some stray bird, lark or gull. I hear
only jackals in the yard, the wind against the fence.

If He's Yours, God, He's Yours. Yes,
it was the shape of the wind. But, Lord,
who do I lean against?

She stands at the basin washing her stomach.
Hard to believe the Lord doesn't want me to want her.
Mary, lie down, pocket your vow.
No angels here. Only hands, soft breathing,
the rush of blood under flesh. No use,

she sits at the edge of the bed,
listening for the kick.

*

The boy gets nervous when I kiss him,
ignores the slivers I pull from his fingers. *Lift the wood,*
I say, *Watch the blade. No,*
you can't play in the coffins.
Yes, you can have the scraps. What do you mean
you'll save them for your father?

He walks through the shop
saying his father is in the chair, the lamp, the dog.
He smothers me with the sayings of prophets. I follow
whatever grain takes to my hands.

*

Red sunset, cool evening. I rise
to salt the fish. I confess,
I love the boy, his chin dimpled like mine.

I wash his feet then carry him to bed,
hum a fishing song though he's dreaming of a man
rising in the moon above the back fence. I watch
his closed eyes, soft face,
slow breathing, as if I could save his dream,
whittle it down to a pine horse.

He won't cry anymore.
Tomorrow he'll sweep the porch
as he's told, check the cistern, fix the birdcage.
He's chosen words, not hands.

LAZARUS IN LOVE

Yesterday near the well I tried to tell her
how it was: like hanging from a limb,
about to fall. We were walking in the garden.
I was saying how my body lost its edges and I fell
through hands into memory, to where I was
a child chasing caravans—rattle of carts,
smell of spices and dung. I saw gypsies
and tiny dancing dogs, young boys juggling apples.
That memory gathers, even now as we walk
past houses and up toward terraces where vines
strung to the sunlight continue to lengthen.
Through the dazzle of ochre, green and white,
I cull shadows for what memory savors.

I have watched her on the terraces with a basket,
singing. There's a rhythm to the lemons as they fall.
Does it matter that I'm edgeless, that I dangle all hollow,
that my indelible breath gets tangled in the brambles?
When voices erode me to an echo off the canyon,
will it be love, her hands trying to pull me back
when all I want is to be the wall,
the shifting palm, to lower my head
and drift like sycamores in the buzz of locusts?
What is love when lethargy rolls over me,
warm and welling? Let it pull me to stasis. I'll follow
all the spores that collect in some wet shadow.
They blind me with their clarity,
the reds and yellows of the garden where nothing
happens but opening and falling and soaking

deep into darkness. I would lean into the well,
slowly let myself fall, but she'll point—she always does—
to the water that comes up bubbling.

HOWLING MAN AND HIS YOUNG

From an Eskimo sculpture

Howling Man no longer roams frozen fields,
at night no longer measures mouth
against black expanse, for Howling Man
no longer has mouth, teeth, snout.
His young bulge from his cheeks
wet, stiff-lipped, green like clay
or fresh grass. They sleep
curled amid she-wolves and lap dogs,
serpents crackling in the fire.

*

A man of quiet concerns,
I go through the day, hands
behind my back, fill the spaces
left by others. My young
are still inside me
lodged between my legs.
Sometimes I hold them in my hands,
feel their flesh wrinkle,
the grating of hairs,
the shuffling of bodies.

*

Nights, a new moon rolls in my sleep,
yellow galleons course through my chest,
black hairs stroke the liquid night
like upturned legs. There's a breathing

inside my breathing, a listening
beneath my listening. I awake
and hear a howl rising to my green tongue—
the voice of my young
shattering the night.
The voice of my young, like blank bullets
at a black mirror.

From

APPROXIMATELY
PARADISE

TEACHING HIGH SCHOOL IN GREECE

I wear slacks every day, teach *Gatsby*
to a class of Yiannakis and Marias, write Emily's
slant truth on the board, check their spelling books
as they carve their desks
with words I can't understand. I tell them

Huck sails the Aegean
on a raft knotted by the
Hero himself. The black stacks of Corinth
remind him of home. Hester loves
the Parthenon, its broken columns with letters
she can touch. Emily circles the Tower of the Winds,
clicking snapshots. Walt hears wind in an Aleppo pine,
thinks North America bigger, greener—endless
next to this thin sighing. Yet he likes it here:
the sunglasses he bought, the postcard
of Diana striding legless.

Truth is, I walk and walk,
not knowing even the alphabet.
Alone at tavernas, I drink retsina late into the night,
but my eyes are wide: This is Greece, I'm here
in the fire of an idea, on a wave of fear and doubt. Figs

brush my cheek when I enter the hotel
where I've learned to keep my dream intact
though the bed in the room above thumps all night
and all morning buses wheeze, trucks

blast past my stop with icons of the Virgin
wired to their grills, motorcycles
race past me on the sidewalk, collect at the light.
From the heart of the traffic I always hear
someone calling: *Helen, Helen.*

Sometimes, when I lean to make a correction,
a young face with ancient eyes
stares back. I'm sure
the dead snake they put in my desk
fell from the Gorgon's head, that I saw
last Sunday, walking through the National Museum,
Emily and Walt holding hands,
leaning close to Persephone,
her smile simple and clear.

I Don't Know the Local

word for that ridge,
    these steppes,
        those tall

thin evergreens here
    and there across this valley,
        the flock of sparrows racing

as if to slam into
    a wall, veering
        at the last instant

up into the dusk sky;
    no name
        for the back-lit figs, the tufts

of dangling grass, this path I walk
    to town, so I veer
        inward

to flint emotions
    which also can't be named,
        syntax felt

as one lone tree
    turning its leaves against
        impending rain;

no story
    to distinguish me
        from the world I pass through:

white ridge of my mother's arms?
    deep ditch of my father's
        last look? stiff

tufts of a self
        I've lost? Am I
                this man passing on a donkey,

two cows with sloped backs
        behind him, one white
                as his scarf, the other

dirty brown like his pants? He waves.
        I grin and point to the sky,
                say the one word I know

too fast. I want to cover this valley
        with words he understands,
                but I can't even gesture clearly.

He points a thick finger
        down to the ground as his donkey
                brays its long

abrasive lament,
        then they turn to a field
                of scrub, the cows

following without being led,
        sparrows jabbering
                as they dive into some darkening

tree while I turn again
        to this unnamed path—all of us
                turning and turning

on local earth.

COVE

Gulls swoop down from shadowed
mountains as you walk
for water. Waves lap at boats not yet
in light. Stones
sparkle on the beach. Morning

stretches to noon,
till nothing is hidden. Cliffs, dark and wet,
rise from the sea, pocked, scaled with salt.
Clumps of earth where nettles root.
Higher up, the walls begin, stones
piled and wedged, terrace upon terrace, every
few stones an upright
slab—three-, four-,
five-feet high. Where the terraces end—
boulders, thorny scrub, cicadas
chirring in one tall cypress.

At dusk everything recedes. Shadows
stretch over rocky slopes,
walls the plated-spine of a snake
coursing through yellow stubble, fodder
for skinny-legged, floppy-eared, golden-eyed
goats. One in the lane, udders full,
paws at a fig beyond her reach.

Night, in the crease between hills,
where the underground spring bubbles to the surface,
where lemons grow, cucumbers, tomatoes, melons—a pond
with bullfrogs bellowing. Ticks and fleas around the eyes

of a mule no one bothers to name. Small white houses
with uncut spikes on their roofs, rusty feelers
glowing in the moon. No one's here.
Hills, stones, paths—all sleep to the breathing
sea. A place, just a place:
no meaning, no wisdom, no secret loves
or unrevealed purpose. You
an absence.

SENTIMENTAL

If I could sing like the *tsamboúna* whines,
like these men at the tail end of a drunk,
making up the words as the song goes round the dock,
how Father's dying and Mother complains and a daughter's run off
to a stranger's bed; how the olives failed and the donkey
was hanged and the Datsun got stuck in a ditch,

I'd sing Patty's dog arched halfway
to death—two yelps, a rabbit kick, then one
faint groan. Sing red earth on white fur.
If I could dance off the grief
like Mikhalis here, arms spread, turning in silence,

I wouldn't feel like that fist they pulled from the harbor floor,
that torso hollowed thin as a shell,
head asleep two thousand years. *Your weakness
is too strong*, my first wife said when she left. *All you do
is want, want, want.* One by one

they toss their bottles into the sea and stumble off
into first light. On the stone path to my room,
the goat, the donkey, the bleating lamb
all feed on hungry grass
pressing through stone
for light and air.

THE PHYSICS OF PARTING

A moment ago I heard the fine
spatter of rain in the field behind me,
water rising, ready to sweep me away. Aristotle

taught wet and dry are absolute
opposites, *each on its way*
to its natural place. So why

do I see a row of poplars along a wall
when I turn, wind prying dry leaves
up and down the golden trunks,

and still the hiss of rain in my ears? I think of the spider
weaving that last night it was *our* bedroom,
rising and falling in moonlight,

not like us but Socrates,
who kept standing and sitting those last nights
in his cell, curious about his presence there—

due only to bones and joints
and flexible muscles? the words he uttered
explained just by laws of sound and hearing? I ask

what law for parting lovers,
one wet, one dry? Our wholeness
was never a burden—then it suddenly hardened

in opposite directions. The web snapped in my face
when I finally rose and left, descending
into chaos, but for the mind,

pure and alone, weaving depths
to heights, mind so pure it makes
wings of thick gossamer and lost

love: *rise, now rise.*

DEAD SHEPHERD'S HUT

Sure, I can fix the broken door, clear the brush
out front, find a rope and bucket for the well,
a mattress for the iron bed in this hut
I've rented for next to nothing, but what about
his coat and crook still hanging by the mirror,
the photo of bare-breasted women
in white shorts and red boxing gloves
squared-off and whaling at each other?

I've come here, a tangle of desires,
more like the brambles I open the shutters to, the random
twisted olive trees up this valley kilometers from the road,
come to lose myself in the deep lull
of summer, to be less than smoke
curling from a lamp, nothing and nowhere. I like to think

he woke early, herded the huddled goats
up the ridge, that he knew each one by its bell,
that he's still sitting where pine cones
crack in late morning heat, the place
he slipped through to death. He's buried
on the opposite slope, in the one bare patch
among briars and burned grass—*beyond desire,*

I whisper to myself. But when I stand at his rusty basin,
see these women he gazed at every morning,
the smell of leather and sweat implied
by their gleaming shoulders and gloves, the ripple across one breast

where a punch just landed, the spectators cheering
from the darkness surrounding the ring, even the referee
smiling and pointing—I wonder

what he thinks of pleasure now
that he's gone to the source. Dead Shepherd,
are you still hovering near your body, or here with me,
gazing at this primal destruction, resenting
even your own birth, that wound that bore you?
Or have you come back with some different knowledge—
taking down your coat and crook
then winking at me with the eyes of a goat, behind their bright slits,
some truth I just can't see.

SARCOPHAGI WITH GLYPHS

"...there are also sarcophagi shaped like human beings...."
—*Guide to the National Archaeological Museum, Istanbul*

Was this one tossed to the rocks
with the babies born lame,
brides who failed to bleed,
or one who watched it happen—
who can say? They had wars, they had hunts and the birds
were all caught, their heads hacked away. Who can say
what they say
these glyphs?

*

Upstairs was a picture of village women
piled in a pit, faces pale
as the dolls they once had,
the spots on their cheeks not rouge,
bruises where bullets punctured
the skin, their eyes on the sky
or the body above
or the grinning soldiers who shot them.

*

That was Lesbos. When I was there
the sheep one evening
grazed by my door. I heard them,
a tinkling euphony. The wall
where I leaned to listen
gave a little as I recalled
that flock in Cairo,

dirty white with a splotch of red
on their rumps, scuttling through noon traffic.
The shepherd spit as they passed,
our driver explaining red
means they're ready for slaughter.
Then the wall gave way:

*

What's become of this man?
He's glad in the dark though he plays with the light.
The stelae can't stop staring.
That he stays is their trance,
tracing glyphs in the light,
tracing our long
list of the guilty.

*

Now he sees:
They'll place his head on the block,
his ears to the mark, then poke
the ribs so his neck juts up
and the blade cuts clean.
The axe will still shine
and his ears
want a sound want a sound want a sound.

*

There's a pheasant on the corner of this sarcophagus,
a hunt on the back. In the end,
you'll all take part, you who mate with a mask,
you who tear with a word then gawk.
So bring your flocks, your brightly feathered birds,
your reasons for staring into the dark.

Come look. Come tap at the glass.

BEIRUT PASTORAL

> "When a man hath taken a new wife
> he shall not go out to war...
> but shall remain at home for one year...."
> —Deuteronomy, 24:5

All day the guns pound from the Chouf.
When a shell hits, the arbor shakes.
The sandbags fall unless we prop them up.
Here in Besaam's garden
my new father-in-law talks
of mists in the Bekaa Valley,
deep grass hiding the ruins.
Dust hangs in the failing light. Before eight,
we go home past the searchlights.

And his words go with us through the rubble—
to be a weed in Baalbek, a stone piled
in that Roman library with field and sheep.
The Romans left that valley bitter, defeated,
to shepherds who now sit and smoke and follow
the trails of jets across the dusk sky.

Home is harsh lights, locked doors,
torn shutters, one room looking out
on an alley of burnt cars. My bride and I
leave our clothes behind the door and go into
that empty room. When the spotlights pass,
our bodies shine like toppled statues.

ANGEL

After a photograph by Donald McCullin

Six boys just turning the corner,
one playing the *oud*, one firing
his Kalashnikov, one twirling his scarf,
all of them laughing at the woman
face-up in the street. It's funny
how her arms flung straight out,
the sleeves of her robe trailing
in mud, look like wings.
With each bullet this angel
jumps a little.

Back in America,
thumbing through a book of photographs,
trying to fathom what impulse leads us to shoot
even angels and corpses, I was listening
to my old neighborhood,
heard nothing that mattered.
Then the garden greyed over
with rain, the hissing of passing cars
pulled me toward sleep, so I lay down
on my childhood bed. Donnie
whistled in my dream—
Come to the schoolyard,
there's a fight!

     That boy's head
Donnie jerked back
and I slammed with my boot—
I woke wondering
at my own cruelty,

80

how we laughed and clambered
over a fence, forgetting those eyes
staring up from the blacktop
where we left him. What lack
and illusion turned that to fun?

Last week,
riding to the Beirut airport,
I was astonished to see Howitzers
hidden in a schoolyard—Besaam
grabbed my finger—
*Don't point! They'll think
you're shooting. You're only asking
for trouble.* But now, awake,
I can't stop pointing—

at those guns,
at that boy on the blacktop,
at these ones emptying a rifle
into a dead woman,
toward laughter down the street
I only now barely hear.

BIG LITTLE

Dawn comes slowly to this departure lounge.
The slot machines are silent.

A worker cleans the wall-size window.
On the runway, lights go out, one by one.

Under the wing of a white
DC-10, a man inspects

the inner wall of a turbojet.
He's lucky to be alive,

the doctor said to my mother
40 years ago, not far from here.

Now the air conditioners rumble
to a start. Shops begin to open. A lone,

impatient gambler
lets a coin drop.

*

Born in 24-hour
neon, my firmament:
The Silver Dollar,
The Gold Nugget,
Harrah's, Harold's, The Horsheshoe,
The Prima Donna. Under dancers

tall as buildings,
flashing garters—
dice rolling,
aces showing, slots
pouring out gold coins.

Then the Original
Expulsion: The Biggest
Little Boy in the World
sent off to return
every summer on a bus,
leaving a sleeping father,
a wicked stepmother,

for Mom
in her trailer,
just home from work,
counting tips at the kitchen table,
giving me the short-stack
of quarters, telling me to come
to the Casino for dinner.

Who was that woman
who took me in
and sent me away
every summer?

Thin legs,
heavy breasts,
tired eyes—the source of love
in a yellow uniform?

Well here I am, suitcase in hand,
The Biggest Little Boy in the World
forever coming back to love.

*

What did we miss, Brother,
never living together? Not your fist
slamming through the pasteboard wall of Mom's
trailer, aimed at me, the visitor,
for tagging along. But there I was
that same night, riding shotgun,
trading insults with a Firebird from Sparks
when a bottle smashed across our hood
and we jumped out
swinging chains, animal-glad
as the other guys. The Beast of Love

compelled me to tackle some guy
twice my size so you could escape.
Bloody lip, bruised rib—
wounds I was proud of as the cops
frisked me hard in the crotch, cuffed me
and brought me in with a violence
akin to ours. In the glare of a holding cell
you put your bandaged arm
around me. I saw in your bruised face
Father's eyes, Mother's cheeks, my own
puffed mouth. Who were we really fighting
back then—ourselves in each other?
our parents, one dead by now,
the other helpless?

I'm asking, Brother,
from a life fractured by endless
battling, keeping me distant,
even from myself.

*

In the Prima Donna,
red upholstered doors swung open
to ovens with gauges and knobs,
a row of spattering deep-fryers,
a diswasher grinding out
steaming bowls and glasses,
loud pounding at a waist-high
chopping block, some chef
calling out, *More roquefort!*

And I, 16, the Runner,
who brought what's wanted,
descended into the basement,
entered the tall refrigerators,
letting the chill work its way
over my sweaty chest. I'd poke
my finger into a vat of butterscotch,
thinking of the showgirls' legs
constantly moving under their table
at break, how Freddy,
the gay busboy in love with a chef,
cries in the elevator, *I want
a lasting relationship.*

I'd pause to watch my breath
hover in front of me,
almost solid, almost able
to be held.

*

A warm July evening.
I'm walking downtown.
The Riverside, boarded up,
still advertises *Wedding Chapels. Rings. A Garden.*
The neon Forty-Niner over The Nugget
no longer winking. The 12-ft. showgirl
with a foot missing.

Who'll tell these newlyweds rushing past me
in white sportcoat, yellow gown,
that all the arrows lead
to great caverns of decay—worn carpets,
frayed tables? Eyes
bright with possibility, they won't see
the tired waitresses, tired
dealers shuffling slowly, tired cards,
tired dice, tired sweepers. Pitboss
and streetwalker, tired.

When they pause from the action
to see their happy faces
in the mirrored panels above,
silent men with pale, serious faces
look down from catwalks.

Walking and watching.
Guaranteeing the fun.

*

In the seats beside me, Debbie, 10, Lisa, 9.
They don't remember their parents' divorce,
only flying every summer to Reno,
then back to Farley, Minnesota. Belts on,
shoes off, they count their change and giggle.
Loss hasn't hit them: *Step* this. *Half* that.
Debbie is a little woman, in miniskirt, thin-
strap blouse, mascara. She pulls
at her skirt, holds the top of her blouse
against her chest. *We're used to the trip,*
know what food to order, to transfer at Denver.

Yeah, says Lisa, all girl,
with freckles, a pink lace dress,
And we got a guardian angel, pointing
down to the city all three of us were born in,
the shadow of a wing
passing over.

CITIES

"Man is a creature who lives in a city."
—Aristotle

My brother tells me, flipping channels,
in Tokyo they don't trash
vending machines, or splash them with graffiti.

Machines have spirits, ancestors
selling baseball cards, condoms
and sandwiches. I tell him in Athens

wherever they dig for construction they find
antiquities: A splintered cornice. Shards
of a floor. A boy's head, the papers said,

with bronze curls. By law, work must stop
till experts come, sift the jumbled layers
of stone and dirt—so a subway

can't be built, nor skyscrapers,
nor underground parking. No time,
the builder usually

keeps digging. Huge metal claws
recently tore through fossils of pines,
a grove to Hyacinth Apollo,

archaeologists say, the name for the flower
there long before the god or the Greeks,
growing wild out of the mouths

of the original settlers—reminding my brother
that Mother called, says she's moving
her mobile home again, up north,

some town called Paradise.

CARBON

on a bust of Yiannis Ritsos

The sculptor wanted to show your pride—
close-cropped beard, tilt of head,
coarse shirt of a worker—
a man of the people—

but your eyes look way
beyond this place, toward light
clear as bells
ringing in the square

where an empty chair
beside a window
reflecting an empty sea
is your poem for today.

*

I stood at the door of your red-tiled
house, looking at your features,
thinking of what I heard on the radio
the day you died: carbon,
radiating from collapsed galaxies,
is the one element necessary for life—
every cell in every living body
has a piece of dead star. Your bronze

face a dead star,
your images like carbon working
in our minds, enigmatic, essential:

Owl. Broom. Banging
shutter. Scrap of paper
drifting by—
your name on it?

*

As for the skin the sculptor
made it smooth yet rough,
unreal texture that would be skin
if skin were immortal. You

are looking back from death
at your tiny island ringed by crumbling walls,
mostly tourists walking the cobbled streets,
gazing at the sea
hung near yet far.

Can they feel your presence
in their own pulsing veins?
how each time you breathe
the sea moves?

PARADISE (OF BRONZE AGE CONSTRUCTION)

Stone lintel. Stone ceiling. Dirt roof.
The walls of this traditional Kea house
thick and sloped to keep in the cool air.
Lizards come in. Goats graze on the roof.
Stone fences all the way down to the sea, and beyond,
the blue cliffs of the next island rising above the mist.

Apollo dead. Socrates Christian.
So the hermit on the opposite slope would have it.
He gives me cigarettes, candied water, repeats
his story when I pass: *Steerage to America,*
cabbie and cook and half of me missing, yearning
for home. Walking the path to town,

I liken my own desires to locusts. When I stop to listen,
the two or three become an entire slope. Listen more
and it's a whole island of scraping legs.
They are the voice of this landscape.
I am the silence.

When I lean into the cistern for water, my face
shines back. Steady reflection, as Mencius taught,
is the way to wisdom, though Hsun Tzu warned:
Morality must be hammered into place.

How would I have it?
Grass wreath on my head.
Arms loaded with early figs.
Body moving in the motion of a snake, the motion
of pleasure. All our lives
solid, consistent, of Bronze Age construction.

POLYPHEMOS ON HIS VERANDA

My cave is whitewashed of course, blue logs
    for rafters,
fish drying on the sill. All of it
    leans toward the sea
that glitters a million gold eyes tonight. My eye

grazes like a goat on Orion, the Bear, the jewelled belt
    of the Huntress, the flight
from Cairo to Paris. Twin hearts—one loves, one yearns
    to devour—I'm the beast
best forgotten. I remember that braggart Nobody,

his comrades' voices like chirring cicadas. I should've
    wiped away some goat turds
for them to sit, should've shared my best wine. But, oh,
    his mates were tasty
as lamb on a stick. Thought he'd blinded me, but this eye's

resilient, can spot the Huntress at the far end
    of the cove
collecting what shines. Crones say her temple sank
    to the bottom of the bay
and it's true: sometimes the sea holds like a swirling

pane of glass. From my porch I can see
    clumps of algae
on toppled columns, a sandal poking from silt, terra-cotta
    votives still legible,
the broken pedastel of the oracle

now a nest of octopi staring back at me. Currents
    wash over those columns
like the *meltemi* scrapes this cove,
    pulls another brick
from my wall. I watch it sink to the bottom of the bay,

as if my heart—the one that loves—
    wants some current to lift it
smooth and gleaming, set it gently on the sand
    among nets, broken oars,
scattered ash and bone, for her to find.

EIDOTHEA GRIEVING

"The Ancient of the Salt Sea...
Proteus of Egypt...is, they say, my father."
—*The Odyssey, Book IV*

Waves keep rolling
and I keep asking
this vague mound under blankets—
why a lion, why a falcon, why a towering flame?

Why all those years walking the beach,
following your tracks with the urge for *you*,
Father, *your* touch, *your* solidity,
your hand firmly holding mine?

You were grass once. From then on
I treaded fields so carefully,
wondering what shapes I took
in Mother's womb—or was it *your* womb,

Father? Did I step from your ear,
a girl already asking questions?
I thought I could have you
with words, Father. While you slept

I'd spread feathers, fur or sand—
whatever was where your ear
should be—and whisper,
Who are you? Who am I?

I'd touch my hair, my chest,
and shiver at the thought
that I'm not me, I'm *you*. Seals clapped
each time you became a towering flame

for the crowds of locals and travelers
who'd wrestle you to learn the future. You won.
You always won. But still you kept changing—
bull laboring up a hill, boulder

rolling through scrub, flicker of trout, gull
barely touching the waves—
each shape flashing before our eyes
then lost in a sea of shapes,

like these questions I can't help but ask—surely
if you're nothing fixed then you're all things,
Father, a *trompe l'oeil*
of everything,

right?—except, for me, a father.
When I step outside,
the mountains are waves
against a hard blue sky. Wind

rattles the unsteady boards of our hut,
while inside, your shifting comes slower.
No fire, no tree, you're almost
solid, curled up at the edge of your bed,

barely breathing. Or is your dying
just another disguise,
that urgent expression
a dolphin caught in nets? I stroke your hair—

your hair—smell the sea
on your fading breath. Let me
be the one who finally pins you,
Father—here, now—

the one who makes you give me
in your dying the answers you never gave me
living. Let me hold your body
to its one, final shape: the un-

recognizable figure of a man.

From MY NEIGHBOR'S BRUSH

Climbing this rock, I carry my neighbor's brush
with long, stiff bristles, emblem of my presence
on this island, desire to help,
to be with the locals
whitewashing their chapel,

its loose head rattling on a handle
tall as a man,
pocked and gouged,
with so many layers of white
nothing could get them off,

or tall as a lanky boy
eager for a pat on the back,
job well done....

Son of driver carries it,
son of waitress, gambler, lumberjack,
abandoned son of priest and nun....
Whose child am I

here on this island of strangers? Stavros
brings goatmilk every morning, Kyria Maria
eggs, and another I don't know,
when the moon is low and the wind has stopped,
leaves squid on my steps. The man who rows his boat
and helps his maimed wife step out

has a life more solid than mine. *A hundred years ago*, he says,
fewer houses and not so many boats,
but the stone walls and gardens were here, that row
of lemon trees, more threshing floors and more
rimathes, *songs from Homer*
and before: their words have changed
but not the music and not our stories
of a lost home....

~

Seven brushes. Seven buckets. Six locals
mixing well water with quicklime,
laughing as they estimate
the monthly pay they'd get for this
if paid at all. A glass of wine
for the seventh, the bearded foreigner
they set to work on the outside wall of the porch.

I dip my brush, swirl it around, swing it
up to the top of the wall, wind driving
beads of whitewash into my mouth and hair,
cries of a lamb from the fields below
into my ear. I stroke each spot
several times and several times
stir the grains of earth, loose stems, winged
creatures drowned in white....

                              Where the stucco ends,
bricks in rows, globs of mortar.
I paint these too, till my bucket is empty,
then climb to the porch, face and beard

splotched white, a prophet come in from the wilderness,
ready to fling this brush, this almost
perfect image of the soul, down at my neighbors' feet,
speak my message from the divine.

Yet I have no vision of the world to come
or its end. I could say my body fails while the spirit remains
elusive as air, that the gap between
one life and another never fills
except with loss, but I'm not sure. And even if I rattled off
each precise step to salvation,
they couldn't understand my language,

maybe a word or two.

~

Wade and I hitching to Sacramento, sharing
a beer and cigarette, no one stopping so we're sitting
in the weeds and he's going on:

You think 'cuz you white the world be white
or you gonna make it that way
with them scrawny fists, but shit,
ain't no one doin' good
'cept somethin's in it for him. I slap

whitewash on stones wedged
under bricks, spread it deep into crevices,
thinking how my neighbors paint their world
white, even weeds and dirt
at the base of this wall—

so, white my adolescent anger
rifling cubby holes, car to car, any suburb
south of town. I thought I was getting even,
grabbing coins, wallets, shotgun shells, bottled
holy water, pliars, flashcubes, snapshots—now I know
I was hoarding tokens of the love
I thought everyone else had, and credit cards
to charge the bitterness to them.

Now I'd empty my bucket
into the cracked core
of that anger, fill and empty it again,
till a river of white
flowed from there to here,
and every parent, lover or friend
I've ever wronged
would float by—

I'd stroke each one.
Stroke and stroke.
Wade was right.

~

No candles, no votives, no psalters' stand, no curtained
door to the altar, all the icons carried out, Stavros,
on a chair, painting the line that separates
Heaven and earth. *Mea culpa, mea culpa, mea maxima
culpa*, I chanted as an altar boy on cold
weekday mornings, sure I was damned. But here,
stepping out of the empty chapel,
I'm blinded by white,

till I lean into the well and see my own dark face
shining back. If I were Odysseus,

this bucket would be my shield, this brush
paint circles to let the gibbering shades
come forth: first my father
with hugs more substantial than when he was
alive, still saying, *I can't, I can't,* Mother
at a distance with her contrapuntal, *I won't.*

Then my companions in the children's home:
Wade, Luna, Santucci, Bill and Roy
Steele—all of us at attention as Sister Leonardo
slams our gritty palms with a belt,
no woman or man under that white habit, just rage
to make us bad boys pure. Nothing

stopped my desire when a hair slipped down
Sister Hermione's forehead; even now I'd stammer
if she called my name, as if I spoke
some alien tongue—and I do:
America, I anoint my face and arms in your names
that will never leave me:
Fresno, Reno,
Yosemite, Nipinnawasee....

Here, washing up, my flesh shines
in the incessant *meltemi.* I gaze down at the crumbling
cliffs and feel the despair
always there, watch the waves and feel love
come and go. Heaven, earth or underworld—

not much difference here. I drop the bucket
into the *pigí*—*spring* or *source*,
the word's the same—lift this brush
and drift toward home.

Homage to the Wheels

> "Just as if one night
> you happen to enter
> the city that reared you..."
> —George Seferis

Laying down his journal, I think of his life.
    Exile and birth, he spoke of them as one. He escaped
with his parents to this city, where I too fled
    years later, from the opposite direction. In his time
whole empires collapsed, cities razed, his people

driven into the holds of ships, all they managed to save
    grabbed from their hands. My upheavels are nothing
next to his, yet I feel that emptiness he describes,
    that yearning for a past I had to escape. He saw,
when allowed to return as a diplomat, his living room collapsed,

front door now a garden gate, fountain crumbling, graffitied,
    thistles growing in the basin. I saw stacks of books on the porch,
yellowed newspapers, an old woman being wheeled by her daughter
    down the steps, pomegranate gone, pine and eucalyptus.
I too want to know *the mechanism of disaster.*

He went on to become Ambassador to England, won a Nobel.
    Was it worth it?
        When he died the crowds rioted as they carried his coffin
            through this city
never his, his body their symbol of outrage at the Colonels.
    Exile and birth. In the town where he was born, on bank
and office walls, he saw portraits of the father

of that new country. Downriver from where she was born,
    my mother is dying matter-of-factly. I wonder at my world
where power changes hands with a smoothness he'd envy,
    yet I'm battered like him, broken by oppositions
personal, invisible, in the stretch of body on body, its ramifications.

The dust of events covers what we've lost. Wheels pass over.
    Something new will be ground, I should say, but I won't.
        This is praise
without hope of renewal, pause in awe of the paths
    we take. I fled my country and wound up not far
from the crossroads where Oedipus killed his father.

Those roads, like the roads of my childhood, are lined
    with eucalypti, olives, cypresses. Here and there
a patch of fur ground into the asphalt.
    The wheels grind.
It just happens.

From

BEFORE
KODACHROME

First Journey Alone

For an hour and twenty minutes
he's been watching a couple
lifting and setting down a suitcase,
two sailors flirting with passers-by,
a woman with crying baby in one arm,
daughter with half-eaten sandwich
in the other. For a moment he thought
how they're family, all in this
together. Then indifference set in.
He's nothing to them and they're nothing
to him, just faces sliding across glass
when the big doors open.

The whole depot slides with them:
tall racks of magazines
in the gift shop, dusty shelves
of model Greyhounds and dolls
with outstretched arms,
bright pinball machines, a spinning wheel
that tells fortunes and stamps pennies
with The Lord's Prayer, even the drivers
in the diner's corner booth, their hushed talk
of a Porsche that hit the Tahoe Express
head-on—all dissolves
when the dispatcher announces from the rafters
San this, *El* that.

*

He steps up into the cool dark
of a Scenicruiser, finds a seat
in the back, watches the last passengers board.
When a stranger sits beside him,
squeezes his arm and asks his name,
the boy looks down
at workers tossing luggage like lost souls
into the Greyhound's underbelly. Leaving the city,

it's the symmetry of orchards he glares at,
smudgepot flames dancing on the cool
tinted glass. Rows of oil rigs
pump out the slowly
descending night—and now this man's
pressing his thigh,
asking where he's from,
where he's headed.

*

The dead were laid out
along the side of the road
in drifts of snow. He saw them
as the drivers kept telling and retelling
their story. Indifference wavered
as he placed a napkin over his fork and spoon,
stroked the bodies lying there,
imagined the bus he's now on
plummeting the full length of a slope,
passengers falling into each other's arms—

But this is *his* story,
so the boy, alone,
clings to a fistful of stamped pennies
and never forgives those who trespass against him.

DRIVING THESSALY

"A bump in the road. Hell, a nice shape,
but it reminds you of your father, where he's buried."
—Andrew Wyeth

South of Larissa
the roads are too narrow
to go fast, too many tractors
along the shoulder, too many roadside
fruitstands. This highway's so straight, so endless,
it could be Hwy 99
north of Fresno, each bump
that one bulge in an otherwise
flat route through orchards and towns, the place
I imagined as a boy they'd bury my father.

He botched that death.
Instead curled up and let the strokes come
one by one, let his hands dangle from the bed
like rotting pears. I wrote of his dying, again and again,
how I could touch the full length of his absence,
feel his pulse fading

for years. Now I drive to understand
why the light here is the light of the San Joaquin
in my childhood, why walnut trees here too
are painted white, why men climb thin ladders
to throttle the branches and walnuts fall
like tears. I know I've botched love,
wanting something more from words,
forgetting that *art only goes as far*

as love goes, so at every
washed out muddy place I'd be on my knees
trying to make him anew: roots for ears,
sticks for arms, shattered glass for eyes
and teeth. I'd want to leave him
in wind, rain and the splash of passing traffic
to die another slow death...but, no,

I'd lick him smooth like a stray dog
licks the placenta from pups born dead,
thrums dirt with her paws to cover them up,
resignation and terror in her eyes
as she limps off to find some food.

And all repeats, mile after mile,
towns and orchards, orchards and towns,
that dog, I imagine, pausing at a fruitstand
to sniff an empty chair,
her tail vaguely wagging—is that
joy?—bump-bump
as love moves on.

BEFORE KODACHROME

I love this snapshot of the boy
posing in his Sunday best:

white trousers, sweater, even his hair
is white. He's looking down

at the lawn deep in shadow, smiling
in light so bright it almost

washes him out.
And this one in his room:

Davey Crockett curtains,
Superman bedspread, Apache war bonnet

on the wall. A patch of light
is spreading across his face and arms,

ample darkness, though,
behind the door,

under the bed, surrounding
legs and feet. In that dreamy silence

before the others wake,
he's caught between two oblivions,

looking up from his bed, smiling,
in light so bright he's almost

not there.

KEEPING THE MONSTERS MOVING

Above our garage a rooster,
a black, squeaky weather vane,
would point each day to where that father
had gone in his old spattered Cadillac
to paint houses, tar roofs.

He came back one night with Dan,
a hired hand: quiet, well-mannered,
but sneaky about his drinking. Sanding the dresser,
he did *The Mash*, he did *The Monster*
Mash. Hip cocked, feet shuffling,
sweat running down his dust-
caked cheeks, he did the dance
that got the monsters moving,

singing the words out loud
as if he hadn't heard me come in
with my bag of plastic army men,
spread the twirling bazookas,
the marksmen dancing with jeeps,
over drums of pitch, piled tarps,
the wobbly workbench with stacked brushes,
cans of putty and Dutch Boy paint.

He left one night on a drunk
and that father came back with Wheelin'
& Dealin' Bob, bottle in his pocket,
singing *John McGrew was a fucking fool,*
fucked all the teachers on the first day of school....

A joke at first, his laughter
filling the garage, but soon a dull
repetition, a vulgar reminder
to stay away.

Still that word had power.
He kept trying to get me to say it.
I remember finally standing
on a pile of tarps,
lip stuck on the first consonant,
feeling like the Dutch Boy
atop his ladder, that forbidden word
in the swath of my paintbrush, and even more
like the coveralls dangling from a hook
by the door, flayed skin of a beast
still roaming the dark garage—

f...f-f, I stuttered,
Bob laughing, coaxing me on,
me and my army guys in a stream of light,
black rooster squeaking, turning
toward impending weather.

DIVORCE

Not her thick, dark hair in the mirror,
perfect arc of her breasts. Not lying close,
with long gazes, silly names
for each other. Not the small, fine hairs on her chin....
Let those memories drift away like dust
the wind kicks up on this island
in the middle of the Aegean. Let that wind
wear me down to the one memory I need: you,
sad father I had for awhile, last seen
in that dingy I-80 motel,
sweating on crumpled sheets, head propped
on a stained pillow, rusty wheelchair in a corner,
nurse gone, toilet running (not from you,
you joked). You kept saying it was her fault
you drove your car into a telephone pole,
snapped your spine, kept wanting to know,
after so many years, where she was, who
she was with, kept crying and apologizing for your life
and mine. Or maybe I need a worse memory:

five years earlier, when I was twelve,
a cab drove up. I heard it
from my room, looked out to see the cabby
lift you to the curb, then drive off.
You wheeled yourself to the front door
(how happy I was to see you there),
rang the bell and started yelling: *Whore.*
Bitch. Slut. Let me in.
I'm your husband. Words

I want to yell at my own wife,
who told me it's over. I must go. Your wife
told me to go back to my room,
covered her ears and called the police
while you kept rolling up and down the sidewalk.
I heard the thump-thump of rubber wheels,
saw light glancing off spokes, pale legs
when you threw your blanket to the grass,
tangled tubes, urine-bag swaying
with each turn. When you came up
to the door again, banged your forehead
against the screen, I gazed in horror
at your bloodshot eyes, the numb, pink
penis in your lap. The police arrived,
covered your legs, strapped arms and waist
to your chair, lifted you into the waiting pickup,
and still you were yelling as the truck pulled away—
You can't divorce me. I'll never
let you go!

            Here on this island I've come to,
thanks to you I don't yell those words.
I let the landscape say it all:
tall weeds with spiked heads
lean from the clefts of cooled volcanic rock
all the way down to the sea, its blue-green depths
inaccessible from here. On the horizon
a thick fog settles. Somewhere beyond
she's brushing her long, black hair. A few strands
drift to the floor.... No,
not memories of her, but of you,
tragic father, showing me how far
not to go.

AFTER THE DIVORCE

she bought me a Raleigh,
the one I'd always wanted,

metal-flake green,
with chrome-plated handlebars,

a generator whirring as the lamp
on the fork glowed. Together we'd pedal

through long shadows of pines
along the esplanade, tires hissing, asphalt

cooling, everyone out on their porches
or strolling Van Ness at dusk.

I'd coast ahead
with a boy's impatience,

gears clicking, our dog snuffling
driveways, curbs, the wide,

precise lawns. Smooth hum
of generator. Steady flow of light

through gathering darkness. Easy
not to see dust swirling up

in the wake of passing cars,
not to feel, so light, the weight

of something lost
settle over our new freedom.

NEW PARENTS

Fresno in August: asphalt melting,
heat waves rising, the swamp-cooler
dripping, fat flies
thumping the glass—out, get out—
and then they want in.

From the living room dark
the boy stares out at wind
clawing leaves across the yard,
into the street.

Suitcase packed with all he needs—
folded shorts, flowery shirt
and comic books—he's ready
to meet his new parents,

Mother Odd, Father Even,
smoke spewing from the depths of their foundry

like bricked-in Fresno.

*

With racoon claws and cheshire smiles
they'll stroke him to sleep,

slice deep into his heart
worn down already, pound his dreams

like tattered flags, pound the red-
veigned gall bladder, pound and cut

and pound. till they get to his birth-anger,
lay a wreath for that wrath.

Then they'll stitch him tight,
fix a sail over the arc of ribs,

a small raft of one boy,
face soft as hammered bronze.

*

When he steps through the foundry doors,
let earth be hard, hands
firm.

       Mother Odd, Father Even,
you who make him new
again,

let the world flow smoothly past.
Let dust bloom where he steps.
Let his comic-book version of tomorrow

be pure as his flowery shirt, pure
as every second he stares out
at bright empty space, sure it all ends
with truth and justice. Don't tell him

at eight-years-old
he's leaving love behind.

*

When the Yellow Cab arrives,
she'll come, walk him out, tears gleaming
on the soft edge of her cheek.

Never again love this large.

The gap-toothed driver
smiles, opens the door, the leather seat
scalding the boy's fist
as he turns, looks one last time:

pines along the esplanade,
wide lawn,
green porch,
her face
in shimmering waves of heat.

Pound him there.

ARS POETICA

(Athens, a birthday poem)

What I want from a poem this far away
is to get back to the boy who kicked cones
and talked to trees and heard the bark
bark. Pleasure his motive for rolling boulders,

and curiosity: what could live
under such weight?—
grubs pulling with their whole bodies to regain
the dark; snakes, rattles upright, heads swaying....

I remember that father with pick and shovel
digging a trench down the slope, the six-foot
galvanized pipes swaying as he lowered them
into a groove of red earth.

He wrapped horsehair around the ends,
taped the joints, replaced the skin
of needles and moss, what remained
of lizard, pine and crow.

Soon faucets dripped a rhythm
I could count all night as deer gathered
in the orchard below, though nothing
stopped our neighbor's shotgun blast

echoing in a tangle of directions,
nor the knowledge that by morning,
hanging from his porch,
buck, fawn or doe. But why?

Because he hauls apples all the way to Mariposa?
Because he gives, now and then, a shank to us?
Because so many want his Golden Delicious,
deer must inevitably fall?

Drip, drip-drip....

Fifty years and an ocean away.

THAT BLUR

in the corner of this snapshot
        could be a pine cone
dropping into eddying shadows,

skippers floating, or a trout
        lipping the pool's surface. In this photo,
more dream than memory,

there's a sprawling oak
        cradling the moon in its branches,
thin light pouring

on mossy boulders, on roots
        in the muddy bank, on bones of birds
in dust the boy always trolls

for casings hunters drop. He blows
        the brassy edge of each one,
calling quail, owl and dove

as he wades the stream,
        then climbs a trunk fallen
from the opposite clearing.

Will I figure out that blur
        as he sits atop the naked heartwood,
feels the scent of mint and thyme,

the thin light itself
        wash through him,
or will waking again send that boy

fleeing down splintered paths
        where deer now come
to sniff the air,

and wolves, turning their heads,
        catch his scent?
Are wolves that shadowy blur, their quick,

easy gait that one
        last flicker
in the corner of this snapshot?—

that instant, that always
        receding moment
he and place were one.

CONSTELLATIONS

Swinging out on a tattered rope
over a still pool, kicking
toward Orion, Capricorn,
the Elliptical Equator,

toward Andromeda, Coffin Corner,
Water Jug, his rope knotted
to that oak at the center of the universe,
the boy turns, lets go,

plummets lightly, quietly,
arms wide to constellations
shimmering on the pool's surface. When he hits,
stars collide, sky shatters—

all the heavens sundered. You'd think
nothing could survive. But Orion
wobbles back into place
and the boy finds his own spot

in warm, feathery silt, where he'd stay
forever, if lungs like wings didn't lift him
toward Andromeda,
Coffin Corner, Water Jug.

He wakes often in the back seat,
dust thick on the windows
through Coarsegold, Nipinnwasee,
and here the cliff-face
so close he can almost read
its glyphs of lichen and moss, its message
gone in the next turn, car jostling,
wheels sliding; no,

not gone, just different:
now burnt pines are ragged *As*,
stumps are gaping *Os*,
tapping pistons ellipses
joining startled quail to squirrels
munching acorns to a doe
lifting her head in a clearing—
gone again as the road rises,

drops into the next valley.
He knows this landscape,
each turn of phrase, knows,
sliding down in his seat,
eyes heavy again, he can never be
that stream lost under leaves,
those larches blooming in a doorless,
roofless cabin; at best that heifer

grazing like a good reader
on a world half-recalled, half-
made up, or that scarecrow
winking at him in the rear-
view mirror as the car climbs

toward the setting sun, switch-back
to switch-back, the two of them nodding,
Yes, Yes, as dust erases it all.

⁓

Pushing open the heavy wooden door.
The smell of winter stale, pervasive.

Lighting lamps in the cold dark.
Building a fire. The boy

shining a flashlight under his bed,
behind his closet, up into

every dark corner of the rafters.
Finding in the backs of drawers

pungent rats' nests made from
mattress stuffing, shredded magazines.

That father lowering with iron tongs
a block of ice—huge, speckled,

crackling in its blue depths—
into the old icebox waiting

all winter for something to protect.
That mother stuffing kindling

into the cast-iron stove. Scrambling eggs,
boiling their last water—

so next morning carrying jugs
up the mountain. Hopping boulder

to boulder. The depth of his handprint
when he leans into plump moss,

cushion of pine needles where he steps.
Mud trembling where they straddle

the stream, jugs frothing at the neck
as they fill. The boy

watching boulders above for snakes,
the pool below for trout and bass.

Carrying the heavy bottles
back down the slope. At the rusty

outdoor sink, pouring icy,
lambent water over his arms,

down his chest. In the distance,
all the snowcaps melting.

~

The thrill of simply being
in that place, weekend after weekend,
summer after summer.

He had a father there,
hefting bags, pouring cement,
troweling the patio smooth, a father

who pressed his palms deep
into the drying stoop,
carved his name beneath.

He had a mother
bathing him each evening
in a big metal tub,
slowly washing his back
in firelight. They'd laugh at a joke
he could never remember, or she'd ask
about his day. He wants to say

how much he loved that cabin, that pool, his body
stretched full-length on the forest floor,
ladybugs swarming his arms;
loved the glass-eyed moose
over the couch, horseshoes arcing
high in the noon sun;
loved that mother who suddenly left,
that father whose fury and despair
made him burn it all down.

He wants to tell them both
he felt each pine cone
pop, each log explode, each
letter of his name contort
beyond recognition—

Helpless as the icebox
protecting nothing,
he saw the patio, the fireplace,
the moosehead, rats' nests, all

the varnished rafters, the chimney,
flagpole and gate, the forest
as far as the eye can see
(he wasn't there, but he saw),
tree by tree, going up in flames,
then Capricorn, Water Jug, Coffin Corner....

Arms heavy with lunchbox and books,
he's walking in a city far away,
in the ebb and flow of fog,
past spindly gingkoes, stucco houses.

He's okay in fog. He can't feel
his footsteps against the cracked,
uneven sidewalk, only the different depths
silence brings, and that sensation of falling

light as a pine needle onto a path.
Quiet as a stream under leaves,
he drifts all morning past porches,
shrubs and lawns. No school, no sky,

no glyphs. That oak the charred axis
of a failed universe.
Still he clings to his rope
knotted to nothing, swinging up

in memory, toward Water Jug,
Icebox, Nipinnwasee,
toward Ladybug, Horseshoe, Moosehead,
Mother, Father. He's ready now,

whenever I need him, to plummet, arms wide,
down into that smoldering, ashen world,
down with boyhood's tenacious hunger,
down to where it all realigns again.

GOOD POSTURE

An infant lowered into this body,
expected to find it compatible
—how to adjust to strange flesh?
Hold it stiff as a statue, eyes
milk-white in prayer, so Sister
Cordelia taught us. At seventy, she tottered
to her room in the far corner
of the dormitory, past thirty adolescent boys
drifting in desire. Told never
to touch ourselves under the covers,
we could see through windows painted white
her diffuse shadow undressing,
our bodies filling with a grace of sorts,
till spasms of guilt fixed the great distance
between Heaven and boys.

*

Sundays, the litany of mouths would open
for the wafer: bad to chew it, bad to swallow it,
good to savor that body melting
on our tongues. Shoulder to shoulder, we knelt
and stood, sang hymns to a Christ
with nailed palms, straight back,
while our own hands smelled of rosewater,
our neatly combed heads like fresh
petals the nuns constantly eyed

—sternly if we leaned forward or backward
or turned toward the girls' pews
meant to be beyond imagination.
Marching single-file to class or chapel
and back, sitting at long silent tables
for meals, rows of coats on hooks
with our numbers above our heads, shoes
and galoshes in crowded cubby holes—
we lived our mackerel days
like our nights, hands folded,
mouths closed, backs straight.

*

That day I stole everyone's pencils
during recess, how was I to know
stealing was worse than poor posture?
I stood erect as Sister Philomena
tipped my desk to a shower of #2
Ticonderogas. Hands punished,
I learned to answer with a *maxima culpa*,
then retreated to the fields to soothe my aching palms
in muddy grass, slumped there with snails
struggling over the fluting of rotting leaves
toward a different heaven.

*

I never wanted this flesh,
nor this particular view. Better a salmon
swimming against the years,
mouth gaping, body stiffening

with these others bumping against me.
The riddle of posture solved
at last, we leap and leap
till we've left our rigid bodies
on a milky shore, pure spirits
entering a heaven
            dark as the habits
                    of the Sisters of Mercy.

Maybe, CA

When I arrived, your gaze was wandering
beyond the tangle of tubes and blinking lights,
beyond the weary, anxious looks
of the son and daughter you raised,
searching the endless white of walls and ceiling.
For what? A nurse poked your foot with a needle
to show me you couldn't respond, just that dull
rhythm of chin squeezing to neck
and back, as if swimming against some current.

*

When we emptied your trailer,
my sister took the lamp in the corner,
my brother your 78s and I
the photos you thumbed those long
nights of pain coursing your body:

You and three men, what memory?
You and two women, whose party?
You with a low neckline, dancing alone
or with what's his name, your first husband,
the guy who took you from that Sierra mill town
to work the clubs and restaurants
of Reno?

      You told me once (just once)
that the months you carried me inside you
were your only time of peace there. For years
I imagined you in your yellow waitress uniform

walking the Truckee River, stopping at the bridge
over the small set of falls, listening to the rustling maples,
their leaves a deeper yellow, ready to fall.

*

Your will made it clear.
No name carved in marble
for you. No preacher or coffin.
Just ashes scattered in the place you were born.

When we arrived your home wasn't there.
Nothing left of the mill where your father worked
sometimes. No scattered wooden shacks
they called a town back then. Just a collapsing
train trestle, a muddy road rutted from ATVs. The town
had moved a mile closer to Reno,
accepted its indefiniteness:
Maybe, CA, the sign on the highway read.

*

And so you returned
with two sisters, three brothers,
the son and daughter you raised
and the son you didn't,
each throwing a handful of you
into the clear mountain air.

The fistful I tossed
took the shape of a mask.
The eyes two dark spaces
hovering, staring back.
The mouth about to speak....

But at last you settled,
keeping your secrets, as always,
to yourself. Some of you drifted
to the cleft of a pine. Some wedged
in the boulders by the stream.
Some mingled with the dust on our cars.
And some fell back on us.

*

Now, as I cross the Atlantic,
the taste of ash still on my tongue, you are,
as always, intensely vague in my thoughts,
but calm now, drifting in that clear white stream
I've imagined for you, just above the falls, where eddies,
swirling with your craving to be left alone,
mingle with my craving for your presence.

Was it fear or wisdom that made you
never fight to regain me? Your box of snapshots
what explained it all away? What remains
is your floating face of ash saying,
I worked my whole life. Raised a son
and daughter. Stayed safe
inside my distance.
What more could I do?

Those words, like forgiveness, its possibility,
are there behind a veil of pines,
the sound of distant falls,
and a sign
for Maybe, CA.

From

In Lands
Imagination
Favors

WITH HOMER'S WORDS

"There are, of course, conjectures in abundance...."
—Richard John Cunliffe,
A Lexicon of the Homeric Dialect

I want to build a house just like the man
across the bay who whistles as he pulls
bricks from the back of his donkey, a house
of words or shards of words from Homer's time.

In the modern language I struggle with,
his words are lost, or broken, a few still whole.

*

Thimós is anger now, back then the soul,
the animating principle. And *fos*

was not the light enveloping our days,
but as Cunliffe writes, *...a person, a man, a weight.*

Stathmós, where you and I would catch the Metro,
back then a keep for sheep and goats. *Drómos*

was a stretch of grass for horses, long and flat,
no holes. Then someone raced chariots there,

so now it's any road. *Kólpos* wasn't bay,
but folds along the upper part of a peplos.

Yimnós, naked, for him the hero with no armor,
an arrow with no quiver. *Nóstimos,*

what's tasty, had to do with going home,
as if our sense of taste transports us there.

Thomátio was palace for him; for me,
just this room I rent, though I would build

a palace, word by word, each ancient cognate
a brick against the loss, its endlessness.

*

How could the verb for loss, *dévome*,
be lost? Maybe Homer whispered
this imperative I hear around me—
ákou na deis, listen to see—and so,
like him, I wake to hear *ílios*,
sun. I smell the day and say,
Símera. I take a morning walk
to taste the gossip filling the air
with heroes, since *kléos*, glory, lip to lip,
tongue to tongue, is still with us.

*

Neró, neró, my neighbor's children call
and run into the sea, then back to their mother
laying out their towels; *neró, neró*,
as if that whole expanse of swaying froth
were just this word, one Homer never mouthed.

*

A boy, I'd wait for each night's story.
And when it came, the weight of her its weight
upon my bed, its sound her voice, till sleep
would come and she would leave a lamp still lit,
a tiny corner lamp that filled the room
with *glow*. *Lámpsi*, I'd say today,
though Homer'd say, *Lámbo*. Which is brighter?

*

Some nights the moon's her slender wrist
against the dark. The fishing boats arc out
across the bay. Soon there's no difference
between their drifting lamps and drifting stars.

The fish all see each lamp as moon
and rise to it to feed a hunger we
too share. At dawn the skiffs unload their catch
along the beach, the glinting hordes all going grey,
their vacant eyes still open, still wanting *moon*.

*

Where do the lost words go? To another realm,
perhaps, a decaying hall all smoke and laughter,
where lesser kings and queens keep nodding off.
Telemakhos is gone. No Priam, Mentor
or Agamemnon, only children racing between
plastic tables, grabbing bottle caps,
playing tag. Homer's nodding too
as Helen's beauty fades against his heart
because he knows he'll never hear again
lefkóleno, white-armed, *glaukóno*, glowing-eyed.

*

Perhaps in their ethereal domain
the gods are howling all the broken words,
the shades in theirs closing in on a ring
of crusted blood, to taste the words and smell
their memories awaken. Only Homer's words
will come to them, the ones no longer used,
like *poiitós*, well-made, while in our world
the *poiitís*, poet, hammers away.

*

Fenggári isn't Homer's word, although
he loves the moon, as he loves the fish that rise to it
till morning comes. He sees the goddess passing.
Nóstimi, he sings, or is it my neighbor
singing from across the bay? And I

sing with him, as brick by brick I butter
and tap: *Lefkóleno. Lámbo. Dévome.*

STONES

Golden Sand Beach, Pelion

In the light of the moon
they look soft, easy to stroke,
have the curves of our bodies.

But really these stones are hard. They hurt
when we lie on them. They won't
let us forget our bodies.

*

When we part we'll yearn
for the nights spread out on them,
caressing the way
waves caress the shore, the sea's
tide rising in both of us.

*

If these stones can be called golden sand,
then our bodies are the blue mountains
hovering where sky meets waves,
shiny cliffs honed
by the sea's motion.

*

Oh, I want the sea's motion
again, our bodies rising and falling,
tossed to the shore of each other,
our gentle touching after.

*

You painted a sailboat on a small, rounded one
and gave it to me to hold in my palm,
feel the warmth of your palm.

*

I remember how you'd roll toward me
in the night, waves of sleep
pushing you into my embrace,
pulling you away.

*

After making love our bodies
gleamed with beads of sweat.

I'd run my palm
up your stomach, between your breasts,
down your ribs,
as if sculpting you
in the light of that August moon.

But really I was memorizing
you on a bed of stones,
the sea lapping our feet.

*

When the flesh opens like this,
the spirit opens too
to that moment
when nothing matters but the curve
of one body in the hollow of another.

THIRST

Come look quick! Litsa calls, and I join her
on the balcony to see a rat—
matted hair, plump, round, his scraggly snout
pressed to a crack in the middle of the road,
same crack some workers patched just yesterday.

A taxi stops, backs up and goes around,
and the rat doesn't even lift his head.
Poisoned, Litsa says, *That's why he's bloated.*
And why he can't run back into the field,
I add. *And why so thirsty,* she turns and smiles.

Two magpies land, begin to peck his head
and spine. His tail—half his length again—
jumps and falls each time one hops and pecks
then hops back. Dark spots appear where beaks
strike harder, faster. One now steps aside,
its partner working at the rat still sipping
wildly at leaking drainage.

                              Stately birds,
with wings the purple sheen of royalty,
tails that bob superior above
their vexed, defenseless prey, they cackle
noisily up on the roof at dusk,
poking away at tiles for sparrows' eggs,
these carnivores that chased the nightingale
away, her all night warbling, leaving us
with just their loud, abrasive bickering.

The rat now lifts his head and looks toward us,
watchers from on high. What dim awareness
makes him cock his punctured back at last
and try to run, though every way he turns
the magpies hop in front? I should go down,

I know, and chase those predators away,
but now I'm thinking of that nightingale,
those nights in Litsa's arms I was
her song. These days I'm more this rat, his thirst
for what destroys him. *Let's go in*, Litsa says,

It's over now.

LOSING LITSA

"...things which must shortly come to pass...."
—Rev. 1

From boredom and curiosity, we stopped
at Adrasan, a place our guidebook says
is *post-apocalyptic*, found a beach

all weeds and skewed umbrellas, a spit of road,
a row of rusty trailers beyond a shuttered
grocery store. Nothing love would keep,

or only love *could* keep. Maybe it's just
these women swimming fully clothed, their husbands
in skimpy trunks that pinch their genitals,

but here we say we're happy, say we planned
it so, as we sip our gin at dusk and crack
pistachios, toss the shells to the sand.

Here the body's hold is gone. Each half
awaits its other half while fiercely pulling
to keep its separateness, leaving nothing

either of us now longs for. What's left is prayer:
Lord of this apocalypse, please keep
our love ineffable and dormant. Let the hours

in Adrasan keep stretching endlessly.
Soon enough Fethiyeh, Bandirma
and Istanbul, a taxi to the airport,

then home to love already gone. Here,
unpacked, we're hurtling beyond our bodies.
Our hands will touch, but nothing you'd call substance.

CEMETERY WORKERS
Zografou, Athens

When the priest begins, they step aside.
One eyes the clutter of high rises

up Hymmetos, and higher, where the mountain's
craggy peak snags a cloud of smoke and fumes,

keeps it hovering right here. The second
watches a stooped woman a few rows down

pouring soapy water over a marble
headstone, scrubbing the letters and numbers,

wiping the portrait of a young girl clean.
The third looks over at the job in progress:

a husband kissing his wife's doughy cheek
one last time, calling out her name though she

is past response, then unties the ribbon
at her wrists, throws in a fistful of dirt—

thick clumps on her lace bosom, several grains
in the groove of her lips—closes the lid.

Two step up now, slip a frayed rope
under each end, straddle the open pit

and lower the coffin headfirst. As the third
takes up his shovel the mourners turn away.

They won't see the workers flinging dirt,
won't hear dirt clods hitting wood. When they reach

the *cafeneio*—by the flower shop,
where the cabbies wait—where the husband

must be served by the cemetery waiter
dressed as any other in black pants, white shirt,

the sound of earth hitting earth will be soft,
almost gentle, like the waiter's voice

as he talks to the silent husband
of coming elections, the economic crisis,

what to do about that damn
cloud that won't leave this part of the city.

ARABESQUES

Hotel Four Seasons, Istanbul

Arabesques in Rustempasa Mosque,
Atik Valide, Iskele, Semsi Pasa,
and here where we have come to sip a drink,
enjoy the view of Sultanahmet Square,
the Sea of Marmara, the seagulls have been tracing
arabesques above our heads, but now
they're diving close to our veranda—

twenty gulls along the hotel roof,
a dozen more screeching just above us.
We see the white and grey of underwings,
their eyes like specks of oil against their snow-
white skulls, feel air their wings all push against.

Is this the way we fled from Paradise,
gulls wheeling overhead, squealing fiercely,
and all the seasons happening at once?
Our waiter looks up nervously, explains,
*They're here because a baby fell into
the garden yesterday, can't fly away.
I tried to catch it with a towel all morning.
Now it's cowering behind the floodlights.*

No cowering in Paradise. Our fears
were just an easy tingling. Death a wheel,
a steady turning back toward life. Each prey
would freely give itself, like leaves in autumn
flaring golden. God revealed Himself
as reeling arabesques. No image there,
just endless intricate motifs. Now all

we've kept of pleasure—the softness of a lowered
breast, Iznik tiles, a countryside—in essence
arabesques And pain: *It won't escape
the cats,* the waiter leans and whispers, breath
warm against my ear,

                        that arabesque.

HOLY DAYS

The priest leads the village
    up one windswept
        ridge and down another, all stopping

at a spring to smoke
    and laugh because I stepped
        in donkey shit (the stranger,

the one who tags along,
    who doesn't know
        but to follow). The men

hoist the icons of the Virgin
    back up on their shoulders
        so the priest can continue,

one fold to the next,
    blessing lambs, goats, the sea
        churning below,

waving his scepter
    through bleached-wood gates,
        chanting some Byzantine litany

meant to replace a pagan rite; he even
    blessed me,
        then the lamb

that would follow Kyria Eleni
        back to the village. Later, Vasso,
                her daughter, will swing that skinned lamb

in a yellow bucket along the sea,
        its pink legs swaying
                in sunlight—how many

blessings do I need?

Traveling Greece

At Ephesus, a guide once told our group:
*The ancients read from left to right and back
and saw it as analogous to plowing.*
I knelt and took my journal from my pack,
let my pen be pulled by oxen-mind.

*

Who would do what I just read about?—
stuff a pine tree's hollow full of needles,
then slip a mirror deep inside the clump
for sun to heat the needles, flames to kindle,
sputter up and quickly spread—soon
all of Attica is burning fiercely.

*

I can't remember—did it really happen?
Did I go to Patras, board a ship
just like Odysseus, that master warrior,
man of many ways? He's gone for good
since now we've traded glory in for fame.

*

On Santorini a cab just hit a donkey
head-on and kept on going, headlights shattered.
The donkey's knees are broken, neck and spine.
That fact—I feel it. I am lost in it.

I hear the gasping locals gathered round,
the donkey bellowing in dirt and blood.
Eyes flared, we cannot comprehend this fate.

*

On Ithaka, inside the police station,
a family, the son and mother shouting,
the father, in his fifties, shouting back.
He's clearly angry at his teenage son.
The mother can't defend the boy enough.
The one policeman hasn't said a word.
He lets their voices rise with accusations,
counter-accusations. The father leans,
grabs his son, shakes him hard, boy pushing back,
mother flailing with her tiny fists.

*

The chapels of Kastoriá have frescoes
with eyes gouged out, the chalky white a glare
of sorts. The locals blame it on the Turks,
their hatred of the Greek religious way,
and none believe this one old man who says
it brings good luck to seed the upturned soil
with the Virgin's eyes.

*

                    Delphi morning.
Olive groves aglow in spreading sunlight.
Chill up close to columns. My friend
points to a sign in German, translates:
Please don't wake the statues.

LOST TRIBE

The temples we build don't last for long.
The greatest thing's to leave no mark at all.
Stars dangle from the nightscape. Memories flicker.
Longing comes, a tiny hum inside
our hearts. That's when we gather up and leave.
Soon everything becomes an easy motion,
camels swaying, horses slowly leading.
We hold to cycles old, invisible,
signs etched in the bark of trees, along
a riverside. We read the shanks of goats,
their golden eyes at terror's depths.
Time does not demand our close attention.

You who dig for bones and shards and label
what you think you know, it's emptiness
you'll find, not our longing's ample flow
still lengthening beyond your careful motions.
You'll scrape and sift till nightfall dangles close.
The outer wall is where you'll leave your tools.
The inner sanctum where you'll sleep at last.
The dreams you dream will leave no mark at all.

The History of Bitumen

An eight-day trip back then from Babylon
to the river Is, a tributary
of the Euphrates, where bitumen was found,
great lumpy quantities like cold molasses,
a viscous mix we'd use to seal our roads
and build our houses, for statues, baths and drains.
Not the pissasphalt Dioscorídes
writes about, what's found in Phoenica,
Sidon and Zacynthum, our bitumen
was pure asphaltos, known for its odor,
its lucid, purple glow, what Genesis
does not recall, just that audacious tower
we built from there to Heaven. The higher we got,
the sweeter it smelled, the more the bitumen
would glow, until it seemed the Is itself
was lifting us to God. The rest you know:
the bricks of tar collapsed. For punishment
we lost the clarity of language. Worse,
we lost the bitumen. No smell. No glow.
As if indifferent, the river changed
its course and so we changed its name. To *Was*
or *Will?* I can't recall. Whatever the name,
it's purple and stinks, like all the words we use.

IN LANDS IMAGINATION FAVORS

"[Athenians] offered her their prayers
and received Pesistrátus with open arms."
—Herodotus, *The Histories, 1:60*

Athenians weren't simpletons, but Phye,
a Peanía garland seller six-
feet tall and fitted out with armor, fooled them.
With Pesistrátus riding beside her, heralds
ran out ahead, declaring to the crowds,
Welcome Pesistrátus home from exile!
Athena in her golden chariot
is bringing him up to the Parthenon
and beckons all to come and honor him.

I think of her in Peanía, the suburb
I visit to get my residence permit.
Teachers, day laborers and immigrants,
we wait from line to line for signatures
and stamps from civil servants bored, half lost
in worlds imagination favors. Phye
is here, or her descendent, shuffling papers,
looking elsewhere, ignoring all our questions,
our seething anger. She'd become Athena
just to leave this din of tongues, this cave
of folders stacked above, behind, beside her.

Now an agent for some embassy
is handing chocolates out behind the glass.
He jokes, shakes hands and pats Phye on the cheek.
He'd be Pesistrátus. Three times the merchants,
shepherds and fishermen made him ruler

and twice they banished him. Fifty men
with clubs were always with him, fifty more
with purses giving alms out to the poor
and not so poor. He built the city's gardens,
temples and sanctuaries, left the laws
of Solon as he found them. Best of all,
he invented tragedy by pitting
the chorus against itself. *Good Tyrant*, they called him.

He died amid prosperity and dithyrambs
from all the poets he'd brought to live in Athens,
a thousand aliens singing Pindar
and Bacchylídes. Strange to hear their voices
here in sullen lines of applicants. *Good Tyrant,*
we sing, *grant us all a residence permit.*
And Phye, so tall in your chariot of gold
behind the glass, instead of tragedy,
give our fury back as tenderness.

CONFERENCE

I'm tired of words. Of making subject
and verb agree. Of searching for the right
metaphor for pain. Want pain? I give you
Georgette, my student who wrote how Phalangists
broke into her family's home, shot them all,
each killer with an icon of the Virgin
glued to the butt of his Kalashnikov—
Mother. Father. Two sisters. Brother. Dead.
And I had to correct her prose, tell her
a sentence is a unit of meaning,
how conjunctions can balance ideas,
colons throw our attention forward: My father
in my first memory is throwing a lamp
across the room at Mom. I, four, stare numb
from the couch. I didn't tell this to Georgette,
my pain seemed paltry next to hers. I simply
dropped it into the conversation last night,
my story no worse than the others
we told, sipping cocktails in a hot tub,
another writers' conference ending.
Mike described his father's way of throwing
him out, how his mother would leave him
at the depot, bound for one new family
or another, give him a roll of dimes
for the Tractor Scoop, and drive off. He could
pull those plastic rocks from synthetic earth,
pile three or four at a time up onto
a dump truck—how fascinating to a child
this occupation that can kill a man

or make him an angry father. Like writing,
I suppose. So Celan. Mayakovsky.
Pavese. Crane. Schwartz. Karyotákis....
Once, on a beach, I watched a man play catch
with his son, then sit, unscrew the lower part
of his left leg. He had the boy hold it
as he rolled into the waves, strong arms pumping,
a single kick in his wake. If it were me,
would I cradle that stub, quiet, patient,
a good son to a good dad, or toss it
away, let him live his own damn life, care
for his own rotting parts? If he swam so far
he couldn't come back, for sure I'd raise it
like an exclamation point, say to Mike,
or Georgette, or anyone else who cared
to listen: *This is a unit of meaning.*

HARMONY, USA

Fog rolls in off Moro Bay, a heavy,
churning motion—and we are in it.

Road signs can't be seen. The sun a dim fuse.
Each curve surprises, then is gone, just our headlights

on fog, its swirling generosity
as now it swings open to windswept cliffs,

gulls and cormorants beyond. No horizon.
No retaining that distinction. Gun-grey swells

curl up from unseen depths, rise huge
against the cliffs, leave scrawls of brine arcing

up shore. The salt-scaled trunk of a fig tree
glints where light now touches. From the bluff,

pelicans drop bodily into surf, emerge
with fish wriggling in their gullets—a moment

not expected, never meant, as fog rolls closed,
our lights thrown back into our own faces.

*

We let ourselves be printed,
frisked and scanned, filled out forms, and still weren't sure
they'd let us see my nephew, till a light

blinked, a buzzer sounded, a heavy bolt
dropped; then a huge metal door hissed open

to a long, narrow room with low ceiling,
rows of plastic chairs bolted to the floor,
prisoners sitting under glaring lights
with wives, girlfriends and families,
their children playing in a big sandbox
beneath a primitive mural with cliffs,
gulls rising and dipping into low fog,
enormous orange sun above the horizon.

Then Robert was led in. His close-cropped hair,
grey, receding, surprised me, but not the dark,
intense eyes and dimpled chin of the boy
I used to babysit. Faded workshirt
and jeans. Worn-out tennis shoes. When we sat,
he kept looking beyond us, left and right,
then into our eyes to see behind him.

*

*The guy behind me's a snitch. The other's
a friend, but we don't talk out here. Goonies
hear everything, write you up just for kicks.
You wanna know what it's like doin' time?
We march single-file, arm's length apart.
Always some goony's face up close or watching
through a window. Same routine every day.
A number determines what mail you get,
what books you read, who you sit by at meals.
7, noon and 5. Tin trays with runny*

mush or mashed potatoes, cold peas and spam
all in its right place. Nights, one bare bulb for
twelve of us. We can pound the walls, yell, or jack-off
in silence. Some nights a needle gets through
and we're in Heaven. Nothing you'd notice.

Some guys get catalogues or girly-mags
to keep them dreaming. Me, I keep busy
cleaning—I do what I have to—windows,
urinals, goonies' boots, even their pickups
in the parking lot. Some days I can feel
someone else inside my body. I'm sweeping
or standing in steam from the dishwasher
and he'll shout, Eat shit, Goonies! *He waltzes*
where he wants, masturbates in well-lit rooms,
strolls into that mural you're looking at,
flies with gulls way beyond the horizon.
So, tell me, what's it like out there these days?

*

This morning at the motel she showered.
I watched *Phil Donaghue* with some trustee
from Texas describing how he was attacked
by a pack of bloodhounds as the warden
and other officials looked on. Folding
jeans then shirts, I thought in turn of chasing
and being chased: first a ridgeback bounding
up a slope, catching the scent on a clump
of stinkweed, along a dusty creek-bed.
Then the prisoner, stumbling rock to rock
across scree, the baying close. They caught me

in a ravine. I rose, fell, turned and rose
again, hounds hanging from my crotch and chest....

The warden asked Donaghue, *Who you gonna*
believe, a law enforcement officer
or this con? I switched the TV off just as
the trustee lifted his shirt to show us
his scars, saw them shrink to a fading dot
as she, naked, stepped out through steam.

*

Should've seen the wedding we had once.
You'd've loved the bride, spiked hair, plump, a real
beauty, Here Comes the Bride *on the intercom*

as she slowly marched through the open door
in a long flowing gown, the groom a friend,
a Mongol doin' time here for arson.

Should've seen us cons in clean blues, happy
as cons could be, goonies shooting photos
as if we all was family. All the Mongols

from LA were here, wearing shiny suits,
standing with the judge under a flowered
arch. We all clapped when she put on his ring,

stuffed our faces with cake, waited in line
to congratulate the bride. Damn goonies
wrote me up for touching her veil—Hell,

I just wanted to see her face. She ran
under a hail of rice, waved as she left,
waved and waved, long after the door hissed closed.

*

Past Ragged Point—zebras. I count twelve grazing
just off the road. stripes pale against the fog.

Other cars have stopped, couples and families
leaning over the fence, snapping photos,

stretching to touch the one closest. We wedge
in with the others, wondering who would bring

zebras from their vast savannah rangelands
to this windswept, fogbound corner of coast,

when the horses from childhood come to mind:
Flicka, Silver, Trigger, Beucephalus,

all the Shetlands on cereal boxes,
wild stallions I raced through backyard grass.

These days there's only one horse left, an angry
Lipizon pounding hard against his stall

when a body I want, can't have, walks past.
I'm calm on the surface, but that Lipizon

keeps on kicking, long after the moment
has passed. Now he's a lion in tall grass

sniffing the air as I lean close to read
the lines of their coats for some hint they know

he'll pounce, tear open their soft underbellies,
chew their entrails in the warm savannah

dusk. Ears flicker. Muscles ripple. We're all
leaning, breath mixing, grazing on zebras.

*

*When you leave they'll make us strip, shine flashlights
up our asses, stick a gloved finger in
to grope for pills and knives. You should see us
leaning into the wall, our butts a row of...*

*of what, Uncle, you're the poet—puckered
lips? Little kisses? A line of moonflowers,
each with its own aroma? How 'bout stars,
a whole constellation waiting for goonies*

*to finish? They check our hair, shove a flashlight
(the same one) into our mouths, lift our balls.
They know our tricks and we know what they don't—
cons can swallow anything, crap it out*

*the next day. Still it's night I love the best,
the other guys asleep. I touch my body
like no other can, go first to forehead,
lips, dimpled chin, along my neck, then stroke*

chest to hip, like a woman would, but no
woman fits these fantasies. I touch thighs,
shins, calloused soles. This ain't about jack'n
off (that's for later, quick, in shower steam);

it's me claiming my body back, the man,
whatever he's become. I never touch
my asshole, though. Goonies own it, like words,
everything we do in daylight. They keep us

bent like that for an hour, write us up
if someone farts or groans or hasn't stooped
enough. Uncle, would you bend, spread your cheeks,
let some guard stick a cold finger way in,

jiggle it a bit to see if you get
hard, pull it out real quick? And what'd you call
that row of butts glowing in flashlight beams—
blooming anai? Yeah, but in whose garden?

*

We made love, then left the motel, driving
back toward the lives we'd left, those fictions we
depend on. I kept thinking: was that warden

on his horse flat or round? I know the currents
rushing through his body—the flow of death
over the flow of life—are in us all,

but that's abstract. He loves his horse without
irony or complication, loves a
clear, simple order. He must be flat or else

he'd wonder at his own inhibited
pity. Not that I would call the dogs off,
set a fellow sufferer free, the image

too rich for that—a bloodied archetype,
Actaeon, no doubt, in love with the dreaded
goddess, his own hounds clawing out his eyes

to lay them at her naked feet. The woods
were beautiful that day, so full of life
amid the dying leaves and rotting ferns

his horse was chewing to fuel her blood. He must
be flat or else he'd go from doubt to want,
outrage to certainty, and feel at times,

in a deep embrace, another's current. Yet
he must be round or else the flood within
or the flood without would wash him away.

Thinking that way, the motor pinging low,
I began to sympathize with the warden,
had him lift the trustee from the ravine,

set him running again. His horse? I would've
pushed her over, but that mare kept tugging
at the ferns, getting rounder and rounder.

*

I'm breaking the rules, I know, by talking
to you. So you can find me through the fog

I write *zebra*. He raises his head as if
to speak: what wisdom, you might ask, leaning
over the page, lips moving, could come
from a body that's a parody of
convict, horse and text, a sign for all three
shifting according to strict laws? I've seen
Egyptians with eyes like his, ebony
set in darker rings, detached from the moment,
like that elevator operator in Cairo
who held the door open and beckoned me
in with a quick, unexpected, *Thank you.*

Since I've stepped into that infinity
of desire between us, let me confess
I love you, oh, I want you. I would enter
your spinning mind, impose on your attention
the figure you've always wanted: the object
itself, without *it*, without *self.* I'd be
You in an instant, if you'd let me
and even if you wouldn't. Always shifting,
never touching, in the prison-house
of language we're all innocent....

                         But, hey, you
stopped reading. Bored? Confused? Or did your body
feel a message, so you went to relieve
yourself of that significance? Pity.
When you left the zebra talked up a storm,
let us ride him, took pictures of us
with our own cameras, heard you coming so
went back to silence. Focusing again,
ignore the golden stream arcing toward

his feet, steam mixing with fog. It's his lips
I want you to see. They're moving. They're saying,

Thank you.

*

*Words? Hell. They're all so meaningless. There was
that three-holer in a Motel 6 in
Yuba City. She touched me when she talked,*

*liked my chin. So I switched off the lights, did
what comes natural. Next I knew she was
tied to the bed, naked, not breathing. Body*

*did it. Went to work with hips and tongue. Felt
soothed after. I helped her with her torn blouse,
found her panties under the bed.... I'm innocent.*

*We all are. Us drugstore robbers, fire-
starters, public poisoners and loud-mouthed
pimps. The truth be known, you'd be here with us.*

*Both of you. No rays detect your guilt,
nor count the ways you done dirt. Now I've gone
and scared you. Damn. Do you like the mural?*

*Did it myself. I know, the sun's too big,
waves all off, no perspective to speak of;
still, a place I'd love to be. No words there,*

*no cons, their ten thousand stories. I never
finished mine: Whoever locked the door did it
from inside, easy to step out into*

*the August night. Junebugs banging a globe.
Old Colusa Road. Then sirens. Flashing
lights, my face slammed to the dirt by cops*

*cuffing me. So, Uncle, tell me, am I
some animal, caged to reflect on guilt?
Fuckin' words, that's all. Mine against all theirs.*

*

The highway lines rush past. What we desire
we leave behind. I see the fading light
and gauge my feelings for this woman sleeping
beside me, stroke her hair and point the car
away from maximum security.

The motor's hum is not my heart, nor speed,
nor temperature. I smell the ocean air
rushing into this inland valley: man
and woman and such a gap between us
we'll never fill it, though our passion tries.

We both laughed at the sign—*Absolutely
no prisoners allowed inside the children's
sandbox.* I watched a con's young daughter tamp
elaborate walls around a castle, saw
her frightened eyes when she looked toward me.

If I were up for life, would my companion
slip a blade inside the sand, or carve a message
beyond that small square window where
conscience still comes to view the ones it loves,
Help me, before this man tears me apart?

And if I touch her cheek, will she awake
and smell the air and see the drifting fog,
and understand the highway's lines are here
to tell us when to pass and where to merge?

*

In last night's dream the cons were women dressed
as zebras, kissing me and tearing me
apart. I was the groom, the sacrifice,
my head impaled and planted in the sand,
singing out my *O* with a country twang.

Jerusalem the Bride. I saw her on
TV dressed in a gown of snow, the news:
six old men crushed when a coffee house roof
caved in, their hukkas still in their mouths—
a tragedy you have to sing about.

So, *O*, I cry, as if that vowel were all
I need to get us through the fog, the road's
dips and curves foretold by signs we can't see
as we inch along at fifteen thousand
explosions per second, and below us
the Pacific's unrelenting roar—O,

I'm a liar without a lyre, blinded
by my own headlights, looking deep into
your eyes, Dear Reader, for a pocket
of clarity, a reason to keep going,
at least a sign—just one—for the next town:

From

THE FLOW
OF WONDER

BORDER CROSSING

Jolted awake. Darkness. Train not moving.
Dirty windows. Dirty metal sheds.

Soldiers escort us and all our luggage
into the farthest building. Sound of stamps.
Sound of power in multiplicate.

Stepping forward, I answer every question—
where staying, how long, who with, what to declare....

And if my answers or the way they're put
cause doubt, they'll take me to an inner room,
strip me down to just my voice repeating

a single phrase, my name perhaps, some well
constructed lie, or a simple truth this country

won't let in. But if they like my words,
more forms to fill, and then they'll stamp me through.

BE AN EXPATRIATE FOR A WEEK

Ad in *Poets & Writers*

Monday
You've come to reap the blessings of escape,
the sun, the sea, this whitewashed village street.

Tuesday
The locals welcome you into their shops.
You're sure the more you smile the more they'll like you.

Wednesday
Cops and waiters look at you askance,
underneath their silence endless questions.

Thursday
You can't explain their little roadside shrines,
why, amid Aleppo pines, you're crying.

Friday
Mountains you once knew, the ocean's pounding—
memories inside your head expanding.

Saturday
That cabin you once loved burned down by a father
you once loved. Both gone. The char still smolders.

Sunday
Blessed be the writer now returning
to his room for another midday nap.

MIGRANT STORIES

Our landlord Captain Niko tells us how
his ancestors landed on this island
two centuries ago.

                          Each migrant chose
a stone and threw it deep into the fog.
Where it landed each one built a house.

The Greeks in Uruguay, he says, exchanged
shoes they made from the skin of unborn calves
for feta cheese and olives—Greek essentials—

and told him of a kinsman there who wanted
to return back home. A bride was waiting.
But bandits stole his money; shamed, he fled

to the interior. This morning the Captain
is carrying a broken oar up from the sea,
torn life-vests. Looking at us. No stories now.

RELIEF

Kos Harbor, October, 2015

Water, dry clothes, a candy bar, a blanket—
that's what we give each one when they arrive.

We put the men in tents along the quay,
families in rooms nearby. All night

they hear the calls of owls and nightingales,
wake to vaguely crafted dreams of havens

farther north. The children keep asking where
the other children are. Their mothers won't say

phony life-vests pulled them toward the bottom
while breakers drove them into jagged cliffs.

Tourists on their morning walk won't see
the skins of boats along the fog-bound shores,

the flotsam of bodies torn and torn again.
Terror this intense—it must be veiled.

TANKERS

Salonica Bay, an evening walk

Crude tankers anchored off the city's port
with nothing but their hulls against the depths,
each pilot house with one thin blinking light,
a fervent kind of patience floating there.

And then there's you along the water's edge.
Nothing you can say, just feel their weight
beyond the personal, a larger self.
You've heard the engine room, its metal grinding,

the silent axis of a broken world.
Divinity should be a part of this,
a presence passing in the night at least.
Instead it's you, it seems, who's floating there,

a man against the weary, endless waves.
Amid those waves, you lift your head, continue on.

HOME BUSINESS

A boy of eight supposed to nap, instead
he listens to the dripping water-cooler

and through the wall, the steady hum of hair dryers.
Late afternoons, when she has closed her beauty shop,

he becomes Qual beneath those heavy helmets.
Steering his spaceship into the closet's alien

atmosphere, he hovers at a wooden box,
scoops up coins, jets out across the street

and into the dimestore's starry brightness to buy
chocolate bars and gum, an ice cream sandwich,

for her a pair of diamond and pearl earrings.
Back home he leaves her gift inside that box.

She could punish him, he knows, but it's
just change. Besides, she loves her Robin Hood.

THE POEM THAT CAN'T BE WRITTEN

St. Patrick's Children's Home, early '60s

Marching single-file into the classroom, boys
with close-cropped hair and shirts as white as winter

deep in the dreams of Sister Philomena
bringing down her belt on some boy's palm,

first right, then left, till all the wrong's been purged,
her belt a kind of dictum, like the cross

above the blackboard or her rosary beads
clanging against our desks—till summer came

and we would build our forts in weedy lots
beyond the football field, killing in pretend.

The dead would climb the flowering trees to watch
the rest get grounded. There was no boyhood vision,

no mouth to fit our silence, and no authority
to speak the words you think we ought to say.

WILDER SHORES OF LOVE

Cy Twombly, 1985
140 x 120 cm

Such presence in this hillock's rippling bulge
rounded as a head that's full of desire,
its browns and greens, reds and reddish-oranges,

simply grasses growing wild. Clearly Twombly
chose this mundane hump of earth to be
the heart in disarray, a place for joy to hold to,
and chose this egg-white sea to form his words
as if just written by subsiding breakers.

Such passion in these letters taking shape,
red and barely readable—they stretch
toward something wilder, something inconsolable,
while we the viewers, dazed and still desirous,
stand with the frenzied grasses reaching skyward.

All on plywood. With housepaint, crayon and pencil.

SALALAH

Walking the Dhofar mountains, Viorel Grasu
was startled to see below him looping switchbacks

just like the master's abstract paintings. Swaying
atop his ladder, body frail and trembling, Twombly

would smear his massive rolling cursive two,
three meters high while whispering, *Salalah, Salalah,*

imagining its summer mists, its valleys,
canyons and waterfalls, the soft allure

of its white houses. Viorel would sway there with him,
holding the master's knees, eyeing panels

soft and dreamy sometimes, harsh or arid,
the last ones lost and lonely—huge dripping dollops

struggling to find the way, their almost-language calling....
Twombly is there by now. Viorel as well.

BLUE ALEXANDRA

Oil on canvas, 220 x 230 cm
Giorgios Rorris

My lover has your name, your kind of hair,
curly, long and brown. It frames her face.

Her breasts are not as heavy as yours, her thighs
and knees not so rounded, pubic hair

not dark and full as yours. But she can have
your glow sometimes, just after making love,

lying there, adrift in her body's repose.
Such revery can be a source of light,

like yours that casts a cowl-shaped shadow
on the wall behind your chair. She's worn that cowl as well.

As for the blue expanse of wall above you, its blots
and splotches and crosshatched swathes that tell us

all we need to know about your passion,
past and present, I've seen that too,

and too that subtle horizontal line
Rorris painted to make the canvas square,

so made your sex, the darkest dark
of all, the center of your body's glow.

I've seen that darkness when she rises from our bed,
puts on her slippers and goes, like you, to sit alone,

dressed only in her nakedness. Your slipper there,
the one beneath your chair, points toward the room

you left, a line of sight that leads to someone
like me, perhaps, asleep while crosshatched waves of blue

lap at his body's ever darkening peace.

TSIP-TSOOÚP! CHA-CHARÁA!

> "Your lamb…: ye shall take it out from the sheep,
> or from the goats…."
> Exodus 12:5

What a struggle, these August mornings, leaving
her in bed to go write at my desk,

but here I am, and again I hear the bells
through my window, rams, ewes and baby goats

in the ravine behind my house. I know
the more I lean to write this poem, the more

I'll be there with them, chewing on wet grass,
that if I raise my head I'll see my own blood

smeared across the doorpost, hear the wailing
of innocents, the Lord's Angel passing.

So it's *Tsip-tsooúp! Cha-charáa!* I prefer,
what the shepherd makes up to keep us grazing,

as now I lower my head and write, *Such joy,*
the soft grassy underside of her breast.

WAITING FOR THE ARCHAEOLOGISTS

"Near the Cretan town of Ierápetra, after a recent downpour,
a young farmer working in his field found a priceless
archaeological treasure."
                                                —News item

After making the call, young Mikhalis
waits, fingering the rows of plaited hair,
her gently curving lips, her eyes with their steady
downward gaze. He wants to take her home,

put her on his nightstand, see if she
will speak—of what? Toppled fountains, scorched
mosaics, centuries of mud and stone,
how she eddied up through shifting tons of earth,

her beauty pitted but still intact?
But no, the archaeologists will take her,
put her on display, and everything
there is to know about her will be explained,

except for how it feels to hold her close
and gaze into such eyes, such deep serenity.

THE HEART'S REWARD

> "We can finish our journey like Odysseus,
> lying on our backs."
> —Xenophon, *Anabasis, 5.1.2*

Whether it's Odysseus asleep
on his back, gifts of bronze, embroidered cloaks
stowed beneath the planks, the oarsmen softly rowing,

or this man asleep on a jet toward home
in love with someone new, the darkness of her eyes
so close, her lips, her touch, her soft bronze skin,

or this other man passed out in a nightclub
parking lot, so absent from his life
the morning fog completely covers him—

the journey is for love and nothing more,
what hovers there, inside imagination.

They lifted him over the side of the boat and set him
gently under an olive tree, his treasure
surrounding him. *His long-tried mind at rest.*

CONSTRUCT

Four posts. A roof. A clearing in the woods.

*

Against the tide of loss, the thrust of fear,
in rain and scorching sun, this little temple stands.

*

No walls. No door. No altar stone. No front
or back. The thought of it what holds me up.

*

A roof of laurel branches the sky shows through.

*

A habitat for love and emptiness,
with no unmoving mover somewhere beyond.

*

Across the talus slopes, on snowbound peaks,
light displays a toughness in its sheen.

*

I let the world around me slip on past,
the chimera of faces, wants, beliefs.

*

It's clarity I want, with just this view:

*

A clearing in the woods, four posts, a roof.

SUNDAYS

"How many men have touched me on the cheek?"
(overheard in an Istanbul hammam)

She steps in from the street and she's the girl
again, just home from school, tired, thirsty,
somewhat speechless as she feels a touch
on her cheek—father, brother or next-door neighbor.

How many since? she mumbles, slowly undressing,
remembering a man she couldn't love,
that day they walked below some cliffs, the light
so clear she didn't even turn to look at him.

She stretches out on marble, lets the steam
settle over all of her. So far from touch,
she thinks, yet near the need it shelters. In a while,

wrapped in her *peshtemal*, she'll step from steam
knowing the spirit isn't flesh, though touch sometimes
brings it close as cliffs in summer light.

#MeToo

Spit in my mouth or serpent's tongues in my ears,
whatever it was, it was his curse on me

for saying no. Yeah, he'd get confused
sometimes, call me Alexandra one day,

Cassandra the next. Whatever he said, it was only
to ravish me, show me his musical,

oracular, athletic prowess (i.e.,
his penis). Should've known me better—daughter

of Priam, proud and vain and much too young
to care about the future, except, as princess,

to know that mine was made. So I said no—
how could I not? For that he spit on my tongue.

Now none of you will ever believe,
however true, a single word I say.

TRANSLATIONS

A PRINCE FROM WESTERN LIBYA

He was liked pretty much by the Alexandrians
the ten days he stayed there,
this prince from Western Libya,
Aristoménis, son of Meneláos.
Like his name, the way he dressed
was properly Greek. He gladly accepted the accolades
they gave him, though he hadn't pursued them,
modest as he was. He bought Greek books,
especially philosophy and history.
Most of all, he was a man of few words.
Must be deep in thought, the Alexandrians whispered,
assuming to speak so little
was in the nature of such men.

Neither deep in thought, nor deep in anything else,
he was a scatter-brained, superficial man
who had taken a Greek name, dressed like a Greek,
learned more or less to carry himself like a Greek,
while in his heart he was terrified
that he'd ruin the decent impression he was making
by blurting out some barbaric howler in Greek,
and the Alexandrians, as was their way,
especially the worst, would slyly poke fun at him.

For that reason, he limited himself to few words,
taking care, frightened as he was, with endings and his accent,
all the while more than a little flummoxed
by the conversations piling up inside him.

MYRIS, ALEXANDRIA, 340 A.D.

A crushing blow, learning Myris died—
I went to his house, though I try to avoid
the homes of Christians, especially when they're mourning
or celebrating some feastday. I stood on the fringes,
just inside the door. I didn't want to go any closer.
I could tell his relatives were looking at me,
surprised and annoyed.

They had laid him out in a big room.
From where I stood I could see
precious carpets, vessels
of gold and silver.

Standing on the fringes, crying,
I was thinking that now, without Myris,
our parties and excursions won't be much fun;
thinking too that I'll never see him again
at our wonderfully obscene all-night revels,
never hear his delightful laugh as he recited
poetry with his perfect feel for Greek rhythms,
that I have lost forever
his beauty, his youth I adored so passionately.

Some old women standing near me
were talking low about his last day,
the name of Christ on his lips continually,
a crucifix in his hands. Later,
four Christian priests entered the room,

fervently reciting prayers and supplications to Jesus
or to Mary (I don't know their religion all that well).

We knew, of course, that Myris was Christian.
From the very first we knew, when,
the year before last, he started hanging out with us.
But he was completely like us.
Of us all, the most debauched, tossing money around
on any number of wanton entertainments.
Oblivious to what the world thought,
he threw himself into all our late-night street brawls
when we happened upon some other rowdies.
He never spoke about religion.
Yet there was that time, I remember now,
we told him we were taking him to the Serapeion.
He took offense at our little joke. And two other times
as well: once, while we were pouring libations
to Poseidon, he pulled away from our circle
and turned his gaze elsewhere. And once,
when one of us said enthusiastically,
Let our companionship be under
the favor and protection of the great,
sublime Apollo—Myris whispered
(the others didn't hear), *Except for me.*

While the Christian priests were praying loudly,
earnestly for the soul of the young man, I was watching
how meticulously they were preparing
everything for the Christian funeral—
suddenly a strange sensation overcame me:
imperceptibly, I was feeling Myris,
once so close to me, leaving me; I sensed

that he, a Christian, was joining
his own people, and that I was becoming
a stranger, a complete outsider; sensing as well
uncertainty creeping over me. Maybe my passion
had deceived me, maybe I was always a stranger to him—
I bolted from that ghastly house
before those around me could seize,
could distort with their Christianity,
my memory of Myris.

George Seferis...

RETURN OF THE EXILE

My old friend, what are you looking for?
After years in exile you've come
with images you nurtured
under a foreign sky,
far away from your own land.

—I'm looking for my old garden.
The trees come up to my waist.
The terraced hills look like benches.
But when I was a child
I played in the grass
below the great shadows
and ran over these slopes
hour after hour, breathless.

—My old friend, wait awhile.
Slowly you'll get used to it.
Together we'll climb
the paths you know,
and rest under the plane trees' dome.
Slowly the hills and gardens
will come back to you.

—I look for my old house
with its tall windows
shaded by ivy
and for that ancient column
passing sailors admired.

How can I fit into this sheepfold?
The roof only comes to my shoulders
and as far as I can look
I see people on their knees.
You'd say they were praying.

—My old friend, can't you hear me?
Slowly you'll get used
to your old house, the one you see.
Soon your friends and relatives
will knock on your door
and welcome you with sweets.

—Why is your voice so far away?
Raise your head a little
so I can understand what you're saying.
As you speak you keep getting
smaller and smaller
as if you were sinking into the earth.

—My old friend, think.
Slowly you'll get used to it.
Your nostalgia has fashioned
a nonexistent country with laws
beyond the earth and humankind.

—I no longer hear a word,
even my last friend has sunk.
Strange how all these chariots descend
and circle all around, now and then
passing close as they mow
with wheels of a thousand scythes.

Demotic Song..

CUTTING THE SILVER BUTTON

Who's ever seen fish on a mountain's peak, seas with planted fields?
Who's ever seen a svelte young woman dressed in a brigand's britches?

Four long years she marched with that band of fighters. No one
    knew her.
Then one dawn, one festive holiday morning, they all went out
to throw stones and swordfight, when one of them cut from her
    vest-coat
a silver button, and her breast slipped out. No one said a word.
But a young wannabe fighter kept looking at her, giggling.

—What's gotten into you, my little friend? Why are you staring
and laughing at me?

            —I saw the sun shine and the moon come out,
and I saw your boob, white as snow.

                —Hush, my saucy brigand, don't
say a word and I'll make you my adopted son, weigh you down
with riches: a sword of Damascus steel and a gold musket.

—I don't want to be adopted, nor weighed down with your riches.
I don't want to carry a Damascus sword, a gold musket.
All I want is you for my wife, to take me as your husband.

—Whoever says to me, *I want you*, must be worthy, must be
first among all fighters, a brigand chieftain.
                —Your terms are hard,

but if God wills it, it'll happen. If God wants you to love me, I'll be better than all the others. Point me toward the battle, the clash of swords, the volley of bullets, and I, for your love, will leap into the fray, ahead of every other fighter.

Yiannis Ritsos...

PENELOPE'S DESPAIR

It wasn't that she didn't recognize him
there in the light of the fireplace,
it wasn't the beggar's rags, the disguise—no,
there were clear signs: the scar on his knee, his muscular build,
the cunning in his eye. Pressing her back against the wall, frightened,
she looked for an excuse, a little more time
to not answer, not give anything away. Was it for him
she'd lost twenty years, twenty years of waiting and dreaming
for this wretched man, this blood-drenched white-beard?
Speechless, she collapsed into a chair, then slowly surveyed
the suitors sprawled on the floor, as if she were seeing
her own slaughtered desires. *Welcome*, she said,
her voice distant, strange. In the corner her loom
filled the ceiling with a lattice of shadows,
and all the birds she'd ever woven
with bright red threads amid green foliage
suddenly, on this night of return, turned to black ash
fluttering against the low sky of her final endurance.

THE MAD POMEGRANATE TREE

Early-morning question
With joy and a deep breath

In these whitewashed courtyards where the Southwind
Whistles through high vaulted arches, tell me,
Is it the mad pomegranate tree that leaps
In the light, scattering her fruit-filled laughter
Into the whispering, headstrong wind, tell me, is it the mad
Pomegranate tree that rustles fresh foliage
At the break of day, parading all her colors
In quivers of triumph?

On the plains where naked girls awake,
Where with tanned brown arms they harvest
Clovers at the edge of their dreams, tell me,
Is it the mad pomegranate tree that pours,
Unknown to them, light into their straw baskets,
That floods their names with birdsong, tell me,
Is it the mad pomegranate tree
That battles the overcast skies of the world?

On the day that, green with envy, she adorns herself
With seven kinds of feathers, girding the eternal sun
With a thousand dazzling prisms, tell me,
Is it the mad pomegranate tree that grabs, on the run,
A horse's mane by its hundred lashing whips;
Never gloomy, never grumbling, tell me,
Is it the mad pomegranate tree that shouts out
This new hope now arising?

Tell me, is it the mad pomegranate tree that waves
A handkerchief of leaves made of cooling flames, greeting
A faraway sea giving birth to a thousand ships and more,
To waves that go out, out, a thousand times and more
Toward pristine shores, tell me, is it the mad pomegranate tree
That rubs her creaking mast against the luminous air?

With bunches of blue-green grapes hoisted high,
Flaring up and celebrating, haughty, full of danger,
Tell me, is it the mad pomegranate tree
That shatters the demon's squalls with her beacon of light
At the heart of the world, that spreads, end to end,
The saffron ring of day richly-embroidered with scattered songs—
Tell me, is it the mad pomegranate tree
That hastily unbuttons the silk gown of day?

In petticoats of early April and the trill of cicadas
On the Virgin's mid-August feast-day, tell me,
She who plays, she who rages, she who entices,
Shaking from each and every threat its evil black darkness,
Spilling intoxicating birds onto the bosom of the sun—
Tell me, she who opens her wings to the breast of things,
To the breast of our deepest dreams,
Is it the mad pomegranate tree?

Liana Sakelliou...

BIRD OF DEATH, APRIL 21, 1967

> Everyone remembers exactly where they were
> when they heard the news.

Did the recess bell ring?
Did my mother pick me up early?
Did I run down the stairs?
Did the teachers speak of revolution,
say it's all so sudden?

> *I associated it with Álas, with Cállas,*
> *with prizes I found in packs of Klein—*

While the tanks were bruising Acharnón Street
and Mt. Párnitha was slowly disappearing beyond the horizon,
while the other side appeared strung upside down
behind the image of a dark soldier
with the phoenix rising from a burning nest,

I learned to watch newsreels,
to follow the parades,
the bucolic life that began
with the same musical passage.

To celebrate football fanatically—

> *One goal, two goals, Pántso*
> *high in the air—*
> *Hellás is rising up;*
> *One goal, two goals, what a day,*
> *spring is forever in the heart.*

214

To keep distances and make minute distinctions.
To hide behind walls that weren't there.

> *To make tight braids*
> *and enjoy the boys' crewcuts.*

I learned to speak official Greek,
to conjure up spells and riddles (always a student),
smile oblivious
to everything happening around me.

Liana Sakelliou...

MENSES AND THE SEA

Swimming in the sea was the high point of our day.

Because of this, without us knowing, a really private matter would get around. *She's not swimming today. She's got the curse*, one adult would say to another, winking. So all the grownups learned when we had our time of the month. And the boys sensed how vulnerable we were to the weather, how easily we'd catch cold from the sea, how much our bellies hurt.

Shut indoors, caught up in this little secret, we played board games, pretended to be miserable, while, outside, that other sea swept away the secrets of the bathers.

Kiki Dimoula...

THE ADOLESCENCE OF FORGETFULNESS

I'm waiting a little
for the different indifferences to darken.
I open the windows. It's not urgent.
I do it this way so movement stays flexible.
I borrow the head of my former curiosity
and turn it in circles. I don't exactly turn it.
I say good evening slavishly to these flatterers
of fear, the stars. I don't exactly say good evening.
With my look like a thread, I fix in place
the little silver buttons of distance;
some that have come unsewn tremble and will fall.
It's not urgent. I do it only to show distance
how grateful I am for what it offers.

If there weren't distance
the long journeys would wilt,
the exotic world that we hunger for
would be a pizza delivered on motor scooters.
Old age would be a leech
on youth, Eros and my grandchildren
would indiscreetly call me grandma
long before my own dusk.
And what would the stars be
without the support that distance provides—
tacky silver candlesticks, ashtrays for bellicose
wealth to throw its ashes in,
admiration's overestimation?

If there weren't distance
nostalgia wouldn't be so formal.
Its now rare, shy encounters with our welling need
would inevitably include
the vulgar allusions of the chummy.

Certainly if there weren't distance
that person nearby wouldn't be like a faraway star;
he would draw near to the primal,
only two steps would separate dreams
from his profile. Though close
the spirit would always be leaving us. But why?
There's plenty of room. We would descend
to reside in our lower, subterranean zones
and the soul with its myth and myth's paraphernalia
would be reincarnated into body.

If you didn't exist, Distance,
forgetfulness would pass much easier,
more quickly, overnight,
through its difficult, prolonged adolescence
that as euphemism we call memory.

Not exactly memory. With a look
like a thread I fix these similarities
that have come unsewn and will fall.
I don't exactly fix them. Slavishly I orbit
these flatterers of time that
for the sake of brevity I named memory.
Not exactly memory. I provide the falling stars
with prolonged annihilation. It's urgent.

Nikos Fokas...

GREY SEASON

Grey is warm, one of our tourism officials
says to a group of foreigners,
*Grey is warm and interesting. Come see
its shades, its variety,
its wide scale of tones,
its own array of colors
inside the monochrome. Grey...*
That's for the tourists. For us

days are like bleached nights, the sun
grey itself inside the mist,
going white like the moon sometimes,
a shade lighter than our hearts.
The sky darkens or brightens and accordingly
faces and landscapes cloud over or clear up,
like when you turn the knob on a black-and-white
TV and inside, the absence of color.

And just as a black-and-white will never
show color except by a miracle,
so too our surroundings. However in contrast
to that which is programmed from the beginning
for black and white, our lives can perhaps be seen
more clearly through a different metaphor
borrowed from the days when we knew the world
by its brightness and color—

gold, red, blue—memories
that awaken sometimes inside the grey,

like the hidden flame that flares up
from inside an ember: it shines on its surroundings
for a moment, then again is covered,
keeping, from underneath, the ember warm.
Grey so warm—our representative doesn't lie—
you'd think it's waiting for the flame.

Nikos Fokas...

FLIES

What's become of the flies
        of nineteen thirty-four,
the offspring of ancient fat flies
        from the previous year—
those with us
        when we were the world's youth—
what's become
        of the flies of my generation?

Remember in bedrooms their liveliness
        completely independent from our own?—
since, as you know,
        according to nature's law
        the history of flies
and that of humankind
evolve independently, without
        interference or mutual sympathy.

Take the day for example
        Venizélos died:
mother cried and the flies
buzzed round our human grieving
—like passersby
        near a stranger's funeral—
thinking only
of their own dead.

Stylish, thin-waisted flies, with wings
        transparent and laid out,

evidence of impeccable tailoring
        over tiny black shoulders—
they compel me
        with their insistent song
        in a minor key
toward some profound essence.

I remember them flying
        perpetually in motion above us,
settling down sometimes
        in a warm swath of sunlight
—eight in the morning,
        across tables and floors—
coupled sometimes
        as if doubled.

Such familiarity with humans,
        you'd think they were
        old acquaintances,
though they're merely
        transient, easy to grasp images
        of a timeless elusive archetype.
But as our acquaintances we remember them
        and mourn for them now.

Truly, we mourn for them,
and sincerely I confess to you that when
        we speak of our dead,
parents or relatives
        or simply those we've known,
calm in the sun like
        this year's flies
—the youth of the world, our survivors—

I confess to you I feel tenderness
even for flies
        of past seasons
—violating as a poet
        nature's law—
tenderness for the dead
        of another history, yes,
        and its lost generations.

ABOUT THE AUTHOR

Born in Nevada and raised in California, DON SCHOFIELD is a graduate of the University of Montana (MFA, 1980). He has lived in Greece for four decades, during which time he has taught literature and creative writing at American, British and Greek universities, and traveled extensively throughout Europe, the Middle East and farther afield. Fluent in Greek, a citizen of both his homeland and his adopted country, he is the editor of the anthology *Kindled Terraces: American Poets in Greece* (Truman State University Press), and has published five books of poetry in the U.S., the first of which, *Approximately Paradise* (University Press of Florida), was a finalist for the 1985 Walt Whitman Award, and a more recent collection, *In Lands Imagination Favors* (Dos Madres Press), reached the final round for the 2015 Rubery Book Award (UK). His translations of contemporary Greek poets have been honored by the London Hellenic Society, shortlisted for the Greek National Translation Award and nominated for a Pushcart Prize. He currently lives in both Athens and Thessaloniki.

Other books by Don Schofield
published by Dos Madres Press

In Lands Imagination Favors (2014)

He is also included in:
Realms of the Mothers:
The First Decade of Dos Madres Press (2016)

For the full Dos Madres Press catalog:
www.dosmadres.com